On The

**Sir Bobby Robson
The Ipswich Town Years**

For Mum and Dad

For those long journeys to Suffolk that fostered a love of the beautiful game

Nick Fuller

www.cultfigurepublishing.com

On The Map

Copyright 2009 Nick Fuller

The right of Nick Fuller to be identified as the author of this work has been asserted by him in accordance with the Copyright, Design and Patent Act of 1988.

All rights reserved. No part of this publication may be reproduced, stored in a retrieval system or transmitted in any form or by any means, electronic, mechanical, audio, visual or otherwise, without prior permission of the copyright owner. Nor can it be circulated in any form of binding or cover other than that in which it is published and without similar conditions including this condition being imposed on the subsequent purchaser.

Also by Nick Fuller

Call Me Bud – Jack Lemmon On Film
(Authors Online, 2006)

www.callmebud.com

Published by Cult Figure Publishing 2009.

For information on current and upcoming publications, please visit the website at www.cultfigurepublishing.com

Cover photo of Sir Bobby very kindly supplied by The Evening Star (Archant Regional Limited)

Contents

Thoughts on Sir Bobby Robson   4

Introduction   6

1. A Baptism of Ire   11

2. Turning The Corner   37

3. Life at The Top   50

4. A Glorious Blip   74

5. Onward To Europe   99

6. That One Job   140

7. Afterword – In His Shadow   163

   Robson's Players   181

   Sources & Bibliography   184

Thoughts on Sir Bobby Robson

Cult Figure Publishing would like to thank: Kevin Beattie, Holly Bellingham and Anthony Grunberg for kindly allowing their thoughts on Sir Bobby Robson to be included in this publication.

FROM THE PITCH

When I got to Ipswich I didn't know where I was both literally and emotionally. Fortunately 'The Boss' made me feel like a member of the family - as he did with all of the players. From an early age he not only taught me some discipline but also helped me by giving me my first jacket (to go with the shirt and tie given to me by Cyril Lea) for match days. As a player I'm proud to have come through a youth system – which he oversaw – that produced international after international, including : Brian Talbot, Terry Butcher, Eric Gates, George Burley and John Wark. He also allowed me to play alongside other players who he bought and either turned into internationals (including Paul Mariner, Bryan Hamilton and David Johnson) or whose careers he invigorated (including Arnold Muhren, Frans Thijssen and Allan Hunter.) I always think how glad I am tha he had Ron Gray waiting for me at Euston Station after his Chief Northern Scout, John Carruthers, had spotted me playing in Carlisle. When you see what he has gone on to achieve you know that he is exceptional. Back then, although we knew that we were working with someone special, we maybe didn't know just how special 'The Boss' would prove to be.

Kevin Beattie - Ipswich Town legend.

FROM THE BOARDROOM

I have been lucky enough to meet Sir Bobby on several occasions, and each meeting has reaffirmed my view that he is one of an increasingly endangered species. A true gentleman in a game where few exist. A friend of mine, Paul Allen, who is a lifelong Chelsea fan, chose Sir Bobby's autobiography as his all time favourite book and I believe his words encapsulate what so many fans hold dear. Paul said : "It's the life story of the best England manager I have ever seen. He took a country club (Ipswich Town) to European Glory and took England to a World Cup semi-final, while under extreme personal pressure."

Holly Bellingham - Ipswich Town Director.

FROM THE TERRACES

The first time I met Sir Bobby, was when he was the Manager of Ipswich Town, it was towards the end his magnificent career at Portman Road. Ipswich Town had just thumped Manchester United 6-0 - which tells you what a great side he had built. However, the memory that will live with me, is sitting close by him, on the open-top-bus, as it went around Ipswich on the 30th anniversary of the 1978 FA Cup triumph. He tried to speak to every fan personally throughout the whole journey and also wave to everyone individually and make them all feel important. To spend that kind of moment, in the presence a world wide football legend and even better, here at home in Ipswich was just amazing, it was a moment that most supporters dream of.

Anthony Grunberg - Ipswich Town supporter.

ON THE MAP

Introduction

Taking pride of place in Portman Road – directly outside the famous stadium – is a statue of Sir Bobby Robson. Alongside him being granted the Freedom of Ipswich and his position as Life President, this marks the very special place that Robson has in the history of both a football club and a town. Nobody walking alongside it will be viewing it as a reminder of the millions of his admirers from his beloved Geordie homeland to Porto, Barcelona, Eindhoven or Lisbon – this is Sir Bobby's little piece of Suffolk. In 2008 he said – 'the depth and warmth of my feeling for the club has never diminished.' As fans, the same will always apply in reverse.

Directly opposite the statue are a number of bricks built into the Cobbold stand and bearing the names of people who sponsored them – mostly fans but some ex-players. The bricks were a product of darker post-Robson days at the football club when money was tight and success on the field a distant memory. Amongst the names is mine. Like all of the other fans who paid for their little piece of Portman Road, to me this is not just another brick in the wall. I have lived through the ups and downs of a remarkable club and, for me, the Robson years were the pinnacle – when our club once and for all earned its place 'on the map'.

INTRODUCTION

Robson's Ipswich years should be put into context within a managerial career that spanned club football success at home and in Europe alongside one of the most successful spells in the modern era in charge of England. This book therefore unashamedly concentrates on the start of it all – long before his 2002 Knighthood and his proclamation as 'the greatest' by luminaries such as Franz Beckenbauer. Without the experience of (re)buiding a small and unfashionable club to strato-spheric success, the rest wouldn't have happened.

What Bobby Robson and the players achieved at Ipswich will almost certainly prove to be a thing of the past - we will not see again the days of a small town club remaining in the top 6 of English football for an unbroken 10 year period (except for one which delivered the not inconsiderable consolation of an FA Cup win), qualifying for Europe 9 times out of 10 seasons and ultimately crowning it with the UEFA Cup.

I am unapologetic that this is viewed through the eyes of a supporter and one who was just a boy when it started. Like most Ipswich fans from that time, I have probably spent the majority of my adult life supporting a club with far more restrained ambitions although it was fitting that the club's most recent brief return to the upper echelons of English club football and Europe was delivered by one of Mr Robson's finest – George Burley. The game has since been transformed by the injection of money to a limited number of clubs in an exclusive group. The investment of 2008 may move Ipswich closer to today's monied game (at least at a modest level) in return for control being passed to an overriding owner and we all hope that this will ultimately be beneficial. In any event, the future has taken on a new shape. To many this means the potential return of those glory days but, whatever happens, we should remember how such days were achieved last time and in very different

www.cultfigurepublishing.com

circumstances – when Corinthian values were mixed with loyalty, togetherness, talent, imagination, blood, guts and inspiration. Much of the latter supplied by Sir Bobby.

My use of the word 'we' throughout the book should be noted here. For those not interested in football (the '22 grown men kicking a bag of wind' brigade), supporters' use of the word in connection with team and club achievements (or disasters) is baffling. They argue that those of us in the stands don't kick a ball and don't contribute to the team on the pitch; they point out that the average theatre goer doesn't see themselves as part of the production just because they happen to be in the audience. This of course misses the key point – that of affinity. For me – and for all other supporters – this word means more than anything. In fact, although I used to consider myself a sport fan the truth is that I'm not. It's about football and then only really about the club (and country) with which I have an affinity. It's this that makes use of the word 'we' not just appropriate but indeed critical. So I use it here liberally and without apology.

I have tried to mix my personal memories with the facts of the day to produce something which is, I hope, evocative for those of us who were there and informative for those who weren't. I do not doubt that there will be inaccuracies here for which I take full responsibility. My research efforts have been based on a wealth of published material in books, magazines, my own boyhood scrap books of newspaper reports, programmes and online; in all cases I have sought to interpret the facts and to add some context of my own.

I have also tried to ensure that all sources are included in the Sources and Bibliography section. I would like to highlight in particular three that I recommend to readers and which have been of inestimable help to me. The first is John Eastwood and

INTRODUCTION

Tony Moyse's 'The Men Who Made The Town' – without question the definitive work on the club from its inception to 1985. This was originally funded by 600 supporters pledging to meet the costs and I was amongst those so the book has rather more value to me than merely its encyclopaedic wealth of information. The second is Mel Henderson's far more recent 'Ipswich Town – The 1978 Cup Final Story' which provides an excellent 'players-eye view' of that great day over 30 years ago and is enthusiastically and authoritatively written by a man who was part of the club throughout many of those great years. The third is Ralph Morris' site www.prideofanglia.com which is a veritable treasure trove of Town information from day one to today.

I would like to thank the Evening Star (Archant Regional) for their kind permission to use the iconic Sir Bobby photo for the cover. My appreciation and thanks also go to the Evening Star, Phil Ham at TWTD and Ralph Morris at Pride of Anglia for their publicising the book. In particular too, Ralph has unearthed some particularly important material for which I am most grateful.

There can be few more unattractive spectacles than that of a middle-aged man becoming nostalgic about football memories and statistics. Yet this is the very combination that I have inflicted on my wife and daughter – Sarah and Kate - so my sincere thanks and appreciation are due to them for their forbearance.

Lastly, and critically, this book does not deal with the years of Sir Bobby's illness. Chronologically it is not part of the story but it is of course very much a part of the man and his achievements. I believe that this is a very personal subject (as is his family life) and that his openness about it in his biographies says all that needs to be said – it would be absurd for me to pass comment on something that I could never ever understand. What I do know though – as do his millions of admirers all over the world – is that the way he has dealt with it is a perfect example of the strength, single mindedness and sheer decency of a man who so many admire. I ask that readers support the Sir Bobby Robson Foundation (sirbobbyrobsonfoundation.org.uk) which benefits cancer research and care in his native North East – the charity itself is yet another example of his courage and generosity.

Nick Fuller, 2009

A Baptism Of Ire

The glory achieved by Bobby Robson at Ipswich Town had to be built from the ground up. When the 35 year old arrived at the club in early 1969, it was struggling to adapt to the top flight following promotion from the second division. For Robson himself, his first two spells in football management had been short and disastrous (less through any fault of his own than circumstances) and he knew that further chances were unlikely. The pressure was on. The departure of Robson's predecessor from Portman Road, Bill McGarry (and his coach Sammy Chung), had been a shock to many and his reasons were an unpleasant reminder of just how most of the football world saw the club – he suggested that there was nowhere else for Ipswich to go and that his ambitions for domestic and European success would be better served at a bigger club such as Wolves.

And yet this view was ignorant. Just seven years earlier, Ipswich Town were champions of the Football League - the only club in the 20th and 21st centuries to win the Championship at the first attempt. Moreover, the club had already won 3 honours (Division 3 South Champions twice and Division 2 champions) in its brief history as a professional club since 1936. Perhaps a mixture of geography and the unique environment created by the Cobbold family under whose stewardship the club had been since its inception, contributed to this view. The truth was different.

Those with a short memory of the 1961-62 Football League Championship season who had forgotten that the trophy went to Suffolk, should however have recalled under whose management the club had earned success. Sir Alf Ramsey's place in English history would be immortalised in 1966 and his Ipswich connection would not have been lost on the young Robson.

Ramsey's reign at Ipswich lasted 8 years and reached its pinnacle with that 61-62 League Championship. It was an extraordinary achievement built on a system of – using withdrawn wingers Roy Stephenson and Jimmy Leadbitter to supply the explosive forward combination of Ted Phillips and Ray Crawford 61 goals between them (of the 93 total) – and discipline that simply caught out the top echelon. Not for the first or last time, the 'little' unfashionable club outsmarted the giants.

Success wasn't just built on organisation – there was flair aplenty as well as is evidenced by some of the plaudits of the time most notably Sir Matt Busby who described Ipswich as 'one of the first division's most attractive sides'. Portman Road was the original 'Fortress' with the club dropping just 6 points at home all season and winning 11 on the bounce between October 1961 and March 1962.

There were only two players remaining of that Championship winning side when Robson arrived. One was Ipswich legend Ray Crawford and the other was long time defensive stalwart Billy Baxter who would, within a short time, play a pivotal role in the establishment of the Robson era albeit not an especially positive one. We can only wonder now what these senior professionals in particular made of the new man – until recently a player just like them.

A BAPTISM OF IRE

Bobby Robson's playing career had been a distinguished one. In the first part at Fulham between 1950 and 1956, he made 152 appearances scoring 68 goals – a very accomplished return and one that suggested that he knew a bit about attacking midfielders that maybe later rubbed off on the likes of John Wark. Moving on to West Bromwich Albion in 1956 and then returning to Fulham in 1962, his performances earned him England recognition where he made 20 appearances and scored 5 goals (including 2 on his debut against France) between 1957 and 1962. Although his scoring rate reduced in the latter part of his career – largely because by then he had changed to a more defensive midfield role – his overall career record of 141 in 583 appearances bears testament to an all round player.

That he spent so much of his playing career at Fulham may be significant to his worldview. Describing Fulham as a 'nice' club with 'helpful' people, Robson made clear that he had both an appreciation of the importance of environment (and, more pertinently, people) as well as an understanding of the potentially consequential downside of lacking a killer instinct or ambition. Fulham's Chairman was the comedian Tommy Trinder who was fond of asking the question 'what's black and white and keeps going down? – Fulham FC'.

When arriving in Ipswich to work with the legendary Cobbold brothers, Robson must therefore have been familiar with their style which was best exemplified by John Cobbold later famously admonishing the media suggestion that sponsorship money would be squandered on wine, women and song by declaring that 'we don't do much singing at Portman Road.' Robson felt that Fulham were maybe a little 'too happy-go-lucky' to have achieved what they deserved. Many may have felt the same about Ipswich and the frustration that Robson sometimes acknowledged when later consistently falling just short of top honours – that of having too small a playing squad to deal with the sheer weight of fixtures – could easily be attributed to that same source of modest means. However, none of this inhibited Robson's ambitions or his achievements.

Robson's arrival at Portman Road as Manager was via Vancouver and Fulham. During his playing days at Craven Cottage he had started to think about a future in coaching and management – an ambition later shared with England colleagues Jimmy Hill and Ron Greenwood (with whom he first attended courses in 1953) and then with Albion team-mate Don Howe. Inevitably all players are influenced in their managerial ambitions by the managers for whom they played (this is a recurring theme when looking at Robson's players who have gone into management themselves) and this was certainly the case for the young Bobby Robson who cited both Bill Dodgin at Fulham and Vic Buckingham at WBA as great influences. Dodgin displayed the Fulham attitude with the saying 'happy when you win, smile when you lose' but was, in Robson's words, a man who encouraged 'positive thinking and attractive, attacking football'. Buckingham was the enlightened tactician, a man with then rare European experience from a period at Ajax. From his England days, Robson also cited Walter Winterbottom as a significant influence – not least because it was Winterbottom who encouraged Robson and Howe to study coaching under him at Lilleshall where Robson qualified in 1962. So, whilst the route was identified for the journey from player to manager, the road was far from smooth.

Entering management must have appeared a dream come true but it ultimately turned out to be a nightmare. At the end of a distinguished playing career and after a short spell coaching the Oxford University team, Robson upped sticks with his family and headed off to Canada to become player coach at newly formed Vancouver Royals. This was an enticing opportunity –

A BAPTISM OF IRE

quite apart from managing the team there was the task of promoting the game in Canada as well of course as a major change in quality of life. What actually emerged though was more of a 21st century football power struggle with similar gruesome results – an example of what seems like a long list of horror stories from North America as it attempted to build a market for the game that it called 'soccer'. The promised finances never materialised – not only for buying players but also for paying Robson himself and his staff.

When a new financier was found things seemed to be on the up but were actually taking a turn for the worse. Moneyman, George Flaherty saved the club by merging it with San Francisco Gales which was already managed by Hungarian legend Ferenc Puskas. The idea of shared management was fanciful especially as, in Robson's opinion, Puskas appeared not half the coach that he was a player (allied to rumours of his involvement in some dubious financial deals). As Robson put in place legal action to fight for the money that he was owed, some apparent salvation appeared in the shape of a call from Fulham to return to England and become their Manager – an offer that was accepted shortly before the Royals fell apart as did his chances of reclaiming any of the owed money. It looked like an escape in the nick of time. Maybe.

Returning to a club for which Robson quite clearly had much history and affection (he said in 1978 that he felt 'part of the furniture – as much a fixture as the Cottage itself') turned out however to be only a temporary reprieve from this rocky beginning to a career in management. The club was in freefall by the time he was appointed and an inevitable relegation to the second division followed.

The real work was to follow in the close season in preparation for the 1968/69 season and, although some progress was shown, it was not enough for the Board which, despite signing a contract with their Manager, sacked Robson in October 1968 after only 9 months including the close season. Robson only learned of his sacking from reading the newspaper headlines; this behaviour by Fulham's Board alongside the fact of a three year contractual commitment which seemed to mean nothing was clearly a shock although Robson's initial reaction at the time was understandably more sadness and concern for the practicalities of raising his family without an income. He said that the decision was about a Board that 'panicked' and in particular about a chairman – Eric Miller – whose autocratic and interfering style demanded total control. Given the fact that the next Manager – none other than Johnny Haynes - lasted just a month in the job before being replaced by Bill Dodgin Junior en route to a second successive relegation, the decision can hardly be seen in retrospect to have been either wise or positive for Fulham.

Robson considered that he had been 'branded a failure' by Fulham. Such a label would have hurt from anyone but from the club that he served with such distinction was appalling. The tears he cried on the pitch at Craven Cottage after his sacking must have represented the general bemusement of his experience of football management so far. In a playing career that was unusually consistent – 2 clubs across 18 years – he could not have imagined a managerial career in which so many traumas could have been condensed into those first few steps.

For now though Robson's focus had to be on finding work to pay the bills. An offer of some coaching work by Chelsea manager Dave Sexton was to prove the key event that delivered Robson to Portman Road. Working for Sexton at a match between Ipswich and Nottingham Forest took Robson to a game between two clubs looking for a Manager so he duly applied for both jobs. Forest didn't respond but Ipswich did and, although Robson rightly considered himself well behind front-runners Frank O'Farrell and Billy Bingham, he ploughed on regardless. In the event, both candidates decided to stay put (Frank O'Farrell at Torquay and Bingham at Plymouth) until they found clubs with greater potential than Ipswich – there goes that argument again. O'Farrell in fact had given every indication that he would take the job and his subsequent decision angered the Ipswich Directors who may well have taken some pleasure when Ipswich finished the season by beating and relegating Leicester City – managed by Frank O'Farrell.

Those Ipswich Directors were a pretty unique bunch and their relationship with Robson was to be absolutely critical to the glory that was to come. To understand the environment that Bobby Robson was about to enter, it is crucial to understand the role of the Cobbold family within it – a family that has supplied 5 of the club's 8 Chairmen up to 2008.

When the club came into existence in 1878, one of its founders was Ipswich MP Thomas Clement Cobbold who also played for the team. When a new Limited company was formed in 1905 and leased the Portman Road site from the Council, its Vice Chairman was Philip Wyndham Cobbold (Thomas' nephew). 1936 was the key year when a new professional club was formed from the merger of the existing amateur club with a newly formed professional football club in the town. It was no surprise that the new club's Chairman was Captain John 'Ivan' Cobbold (formerly President of the amateur club) and one of its Directors was Major Robert Nevill Cobbold (son of Philip). It only took a further two years for the club to be elected to the Football League but its initial playing term was cut short by war during which its debts might have ended the club before it had begun were it not for the generosity of Captain Ivan in clearing them.

Philip was once again restored to the club to oversee the resumption of football after the war – both Ivan and Robert having been tragically killed in action. This resumed involvement in the club was itself truncated when Philip died aged 70 but the Cobbold family's association was far from over. First his son Alistair joined the Board (later to become Chairman in 1949) and then Ivan's son John joined him (also to subsequently become Chairman in 1957 – at the time the youngest in the country at just 29). Captain Ivan's widow, Lady Blanche, also became an Honorary President in 1965 one year after John's brother, Patrick, joined the Board.

Patrick took over as Chairman from his brother in 1976 and it was this partnership of brothers that is most associated with the appointment, support and nurturing of Bobby Robson. A glowing mutual respect is evident in every word uttered by all three about each other.

As critical and colourful as the Cobbold's role is in the story of Ipswich Town, they are not the central characters. They did not believe that they should be. In this day and age when club owners and Chairmen often seem intent on taking the limelight as much as the players and management, it may be hard to understand that the Cobbolds saw their role as supportive. Robson knew this – he knew that they would 'let a manager manage'.

There are innumerable stories of the brothers' exploits (most comprehensively chronicled in Brian Scovell's book 'Football Gentry') but they were never undertaken in the glare of publicity. Since the tabloids were not so intent on discovering quotable characters, maybe the temptation wasn't there but the fact was that the Cobbold's didn't live for other people – they lived for themselves. Their eccentricities were their own. Their passion for the football club and their support of its

A BAPTISM OF IRE

management was based on their own creed. The most important manifestation of this of course would turn out to be their support of managers when things went wrong. For many Directors and Chairmen, if ever there is a time to wade towards the spotlight brandishing the axe and a promise of a new dawn under their stewardship it is when results are going the wrong way. The Cobbolds didn't think like that.

The relationship that was so much the foundation of the club's achievements under Robson was to bloom over 13 years but, right at the outset, it needed a helping hand. Unbeknownst to Robson, both Bertie Mee and Dave Sexton had provided the Ipswich Board with glowing references for the young Robson. This, combined with a forthright interview in January 1969 with John Cobbold and fellow Directors Ken Brightwell and Harold Smith, persuaded Ipswich to take a chance on the young and inexperienced Robson. Cobbold's statement to the press announcing the appointment was refreshingly straightforward by today's standards. He described the Board as 'vastly impressed' with Robson and avowed 'that there was no doubt in our minds that he was the right man for the job'. In Cobbold's words, Robson was 'obviously pretty tough but most pleasant' (a rare word in the lexicon of football these days) and his 'whole life is bound up with football'.

There may have been some scepticism around Suffolk that this was the cheap option or even the only one (such odd sentiments were expressed when Jim Magilton took over the reins almost 40 years later) but the truth is more likely simply that both parties had identified the right mix.

No one doubted that the job was a tough one. Ex-Manager Jackie Milburn (who had succeeded Sir Alf Ramsay at Portman Road) acknowledged Bill McGarry's reasons for heading for Wolves. He said at the time of Robson's appointment that 'Bill

McGarry said he had got every ounce from his team. Since they are fifth from bottom of the table at present I would say they have only one way to go – and that is down. At best the Ipswich area can accommodate only a second division side'. Quite what Milburn made of the next 13 years in particular (and quite a few after that) is not recorded.

The deal itself had one unusual attribute which may have played a part in the Board's decision – there was no contract but rather a handshake from the Cobbolds committing Robson to at least two years in the job! Given Robson's very recent experience with contracts at Fulham, the lack of one here may not have been the concern that it might appear although he's recorded as wondering what would happen when he struggled for results. Maybe the value of a 'gentlemanly handshake' at a decent football club was a very real bonus that he was about to discover.

Robson believed so. He told the BBC on his appointment that – 'I've come here because I know, from my own personal point of view and as far as my own working conditions are concerned, that this is a club which will allow me to manage and is prepared to give me a chance'. Indeed, Patrick Cobbold later put it possibly even stronger – 'if you appoint a manager you must let him manage....everything'. The Ipswich Board had not only taken a risk but also made a complete commitment by entrusting the club – on and off the field – to a young and passionate Geordie at the bottom of the managerial ladder.

****

Something of a clearout was in the air when Robson arrived at Portman Road. Danny Hegan, John O'Rourke and Peter Morris were already on the transfer list at their own request and key striker Ray Crawford had privately agreed with John Cobbold to move on and finish playing at a lower level in South Africa after an extraordinary career for Ipswich. Crawford himself considered Robson's job a tough one and remembers the days after Bill McGarry's departure being defined by 'silence everywhere from the dressing room to the training ground'. Worse, in his view, was that the players felt that 'all the passion for the game and the intense desire to win' that McGarry had instilled in the team had left with him.

According to Crawford, despite the Chairman's verbal agreement, Robson and the Board stood in the way of Crawford's departure. The assumption is that they wanted to ensure the maximum revenue for the departing player whilst also probably eyeing up a youthful replacement. Crawford was understandably unhappy both at the outcome and the fact that Robson didn't speak to him during the uncertain times before the decision was made to place him on the transfer list rather than releasing him on a free; as a consequence the move to South Africa bit the dust and Crawford's life plans were thrown into turmoil. There could have been few more significant player developments in Robson's early weeks – to this day Crawford remains the club's top scorer with 227 goals in 2 spells totalling 8 years.

The Crawford situation became public and some local correspondents aired their concern over the way that the club had treated him. It does seem odd that the legendary old Etonian Cobbold way could have been overturned. The 'gentlemanly handshake' didn't seem to work so well here.

The obvious suspicion was that Robson was the architect of the turn around and certainly Crawford considered the young manager to have a lot to learn about man management in the way that the situation was handled. It seems hard to believe that Robson hadn't done the most basic of research to realise the massive contribution made by Crawford – maybe Robson was simply being financially pragmatic and putting aside sentiment. Balancing the books was one of his long terms successes at Ipswich that is often less reported than on the field achievements.

Most importantly, Crawford's contribution was very current as the striker hit his 17th goal of the season in a 2-0 win at Highbury in Robson's second month at the club. Despite eventually leaving with around a quarter of the season still to play, Crawford still ended the season as joint top scorer. After joining Charlton he returned to Portman Road for an end of season testimonial against Bill McGarry's Wolves in front of almost 17,000 appreciative fans. Crawford's career was far from over – a subsequent hat-trick while at Colchester gave him the record of the first player to score hat-tricks in the League, FA Cup, League Cup and European Cup. The word 'legend' should have Ray Crawford's picture next to it in the dictionary.

Hegan was a loss too. He had been almost an ever present over the previous 4 seasons and always weighed in with his share of goals. Although he did move on, Hegan's departure (to WBA with Ian Collard joining Ipswich as part of the deal as Robson's first cash signing) was delayed until after the final game of 1968/69 enabling him to contribute 38 appearances although just 3 goals.

The focus of Robson's early days was clearly on steadying the ship. With such a list of impending departures, a poor league position and, at least for some, the atmosphere of scepticism about the young Manager, results mattered more than anything. Robson sold goalkeeper Ken Hancock to Tottenham but did little else in the transfer market and yet his initial impact was significant because the side finished a creditable 12th and lost only 4 games between Robson's arrival and the season's end. This was achieved with largely the same playing staff and the

Manager ensured similar continuity by retaining the services of Cyril Lea in a new coaching role (in addition to his registration as a player.) He also bought in additional coaching skills in the form of Roy McCrohan who followed him from Fulham.

Given the turbulence of his managerial baptism at Fulham and Vancouver, Robson must have allowed himself some pause for satisfaction at the league position in May 1969. If however, he felt that he had established himself at Portman Road he was in for a shock. Now that his rebuilding programme was about to begin, there would be further troubles to come from which he knew there would be no hiding.

****

1969/70 would turn out to be a troubled but extremely significant season both for the young manager and for his new club.

Any end of season enthusiasm that may have remained in the air come August as the new one kicked off was quickly dispelled. Ipswich failed to win in their first 5 games and scored just one goal. Before the season had started, Bobby Houghton had departed and, a third of the way through, John O'Rourke followed him. O'Rourke had been near ever present in the previous season and his goal haul equalled Crawford's so that 32 of the 59 goals scored the previous season were by players no longer wearing a blue shirt in 1969/70.

Goals would inevitably be a problem - whatever plan Robson had to replace the Crawford/O'Rourke axis from existing staff did not pay off and it was the twin signing of Frank Clarke from QPR and Jimmy Robertson from Arsenal that finally did the trick at the 11th hour – both were signed just seven games from the end of the season and their five goals proved decisive.

The double signing was inspired. Ten years later Robson recalled his pride at landing two quality players and his gratitude to the Board for releasing the £100,000 necessary. He saw them as 'very important to the club's development' and you can see why. The signings too were an equally important illustration of Robson's judgement and decisiveness as well as the Board's recognition of such values and its support for him.

Robson's first full season had however delivered a relatively poor final result – 18th place was well clear of the relegation mire but compared poorly with the previous two seasons. Double signing aside, the supporters were struggling to see where the next heroes were coming from.

Indeed, there were many doubters who concentrated more on the sales that caused the goal drought than the buys that solved it. Whilst it may not yet have been public, the festering relationship between Robson and Town legend Billy Baxter was also to become a focus of this discontent. The esteem in which the Suffolk public held Baxter could be measured by a 16,000 crowd that turned out for his Testimonial match. It's reasonable to surmise that there were a fair number of doubters about the manager in the crowd that night and that, had they known of the oncoming clash between the two, Robson's corner might have looked rather more threadbare by comparison.

For now, Robson was focussed on trying to create a unit able to move the club on. He needed players who wanted to be there and would adapt to the new manager's plan. Changes were necessary and the supporters were looking for them too.

One incident, recalled by Trevor Whymark thirty five years later, casts a revealing light on the way that the game has changed and, in particular, the increased role of the media as the 'eyes and ears' of the supporter. Whymark recalled as decisive a meeting called by Robson of 17 of the squad at which he made clear that this was the group that he saw as being critical in pulling the club through the relegation battle. For Whymark – like the other 16 presumably – it 'lifted morale' knowing that Robson had 'sufficient belief' in him. In 2008 a similar meeting is reputed to have happened but the press and supporters alike suggested that its selective nature was damaging to the morale of the squad as a whole. The parallel is obvious even if the intentions (or maybe even the events themselves) were not. It's a thin line between inspiration and vilification in football management – often drawn by the omnipresent media.

****

For an eight year old living in Kent, Ipswich Town was not the most obvious choice of footballing affiliations. The club was barely on the map. The 'big clubs' (primarily Leeds, Liverpool, Arsenal, Everton and Chelsea who consistently vied for the top honours during that period - occasionally joined by interlopers such as Derby and Spurs) then – as now – hogged the limelight. Media coverage too was unimaginably limited compared to today so there was little to persuade the unaffiliated youngster that a Suffolk club might compete on glamour when it came to playground positioning.

Maybe I saw something in what was being built at Ipswich. More likely this is just flattering myself. The explanation was probably much simpler in that I was trying to avoid the crowd. I'm ashamed to say that I did have momentary dalliances with Leeds and Arsenal but they were just transitory infatuations. There were aspects of both clubs that I just couldn't stand – for instance the Big Time Charlies of Arsenal or the dour (and, in retrospect, downright violent) efficiency of Leeds.

The real life long love affair started there and then. As was pointed out to me pretty much daily both then and later,

Ipswich wasn't a 'real' football club. Arsenal supporters at school later derided the initials ITFC as being substandard graffiti – how could a football club be taken seriously when it started with an 'I'! To them no doubt Ipswich had never achieved anything – when you are an 8-year-old, a League Championship won eight years ago seems positively prehistoric.

The opinion of your peers is pretty damned important as a football obsessed 8-year-old. I had been bitten by the football bug and it had taken over pretty much every waking moment. I played (at a pretty consistently average standard) at school, at home, at cubs, after school and probably – if I could have got away with it – instead of school too.

I have clear memories of two football teachers at Primary School – one (a Welshman named Mr Thomas) whose sole coaching consisted of yelling the word 'shoot' whenever anyone in our team had the ball in whatever position at whatever time in the game. The other (whose name escapes me) focussed more on defence by repeating his mantra 'if in doubt, kick it out'. I often wondered whether this latter advice had any relationship to the shocking inability of British born defenders to do much more than lump clearances into Row Z. Many years later on a trip to Italy for the Milan derby, the greatest revelation for me (beyond the noise and the scale) was acknowledgement that some defenders can trap the ball, look up and spray 40 yard passes to their team-mates.

Like most kids, the game needed no glamour to keep us interested – we played with a tennis ball in the street and, even at school, our changing room was an ex-world war two bunker which was notoriously dank and uncomfortable but nobody cared (although, thinking about it now, maybe we actually thought that pretty cool).

My own obsession was sometimes unhealthy. I remember once that a game I was playing in against another local school was moved from an after school to an early afternoon kick off. So keen was I to get the message to my dad in order that he could be there to watch it (assuming of course that he'd immediately rearrange his day around this event) that I rushed home at lunch time to pass on the news. Unfortunately neither he nor my mum was around. Using my initiative therefore I managed to carve a message (something succinct like 'kick off 2PM. See you later') into the wooden door of our shed. Clearly I viewed this as a matter of the utmost importance that warranted whatever communication method was available. My mum and dad however didn't quite see it that way and were less than amused at having this permanent momento preserved for posterity for all to see. What we would have done for a mobile in those days.

If I wasn't playing, I was watching. Our diet of football was delivered via Match Of The Day (traditionally a late-at-night treat for one so young) and, far more importantly, Sunday afternoon ITV programme 'The Big Match.' The latter was a staple throughout my childhood. After watching the programme, come rain or shine, I would immediately escape into our backyard with a tennis ball and enact the marvellous goals that I would inevitably start to score as I became Ipswich's – and England's – leading forward.

Imagination has no limitation at that age of course – the small square of garden and the breeze blocks against which the tennis ball is hammered can be just as inspiring as Wembley Stadium itself when you are sufficiently intoxicated. In fact my career was mapped out. I would start at non League Tonbridge as this was both my nearest semi-pro club (i.e. one with a ground and floodlights!) and the club at which I saw my first game. My dad had been a regular there with his dad and his cousins, all of whom had grown up on real live football with proper affiliations – a feeling that seems to have become ever rarer as the generations have progressed.

As exciting though it was to visit the old Angel Ground (now long since replaced by a concrete monstrosity Sainsbury's – despite the collection of a petition by myself and one or two other hardy teenagers at the time), I knew that my destiny lay farther afield and that my career was therefore all about getting to Ipswich as soon as possible.

These day dreams were fuelled by the telly. 'The Big Match' was presented by Brian Moore who (in the words of the song) had a head that was 'uncannily like the London Planetarium'. Brian was our sage. Joined by Jimmy Hill and, sometimes, Brian Clough, he would be the constant through years of changing football fortunes and fashions; the voice of continuity between ego's clashing. He was however a Gillingham supporter and, far more importantly, The Big Match was a regional programme so its choice of games reflected the viewer's location.

In Kent we were close enough – where it suited – to be considered almost Londoners hence the Arsenal and Chelsea scarves (replica shirts were a rarity then) at school and the single minded view of TV presenting. There was therefore little mention of clubs outside of London and/or the top First Division positions; Ipswich? – never heard of them. The only exception was when some of the lesser and unfashionable clubs were afforded the honour of visiting Stamford Bridge or Highbury just as long as they remembered their place and went home pointless and suitably chastised. And that's the way it generally was – beating the big boys was a rarity but one to be sampled with even greater delight because of it.

There was however a ray of hope. Jimmy Robertson was the first 'star' that I remember in an Ipswich shirt. The likes of Phillips and Crawford were before my time but, in any case, the game was changing and Charlie George, George Best, Rodney Marsh and Stan Bowles were the icons of the day. These players had something else. As well as being star performers, they had a flair that transcended what they did and focussed on how they did it; both on and off the pitch they had an aura. Now it looked as though we had our icon. So when it came to playground matches, whilst the others all wanted to 'be' the names of the day I determined to 'be' Mr Robertson, the flying winger whose arrival at Ipswich had turned around a season – maybe not to win a trophy but certainly to deliver a more hopeful future.

****

Five games in to 1970/71 and hope was about all that we had to hang on to. Bottom of the League and goalless, any talk of a Robson Revolution would have been seen as mad. A first League win didn't come until early September – a contender for a relegation six pointer with Burnley who would continue to struggle and ultimately fall at the end of the season – when goals from Clarke and Billy Baxter at last bought a little relief.

Baxter was a pivotal figure. His 409 league appearance haul was, at the time, just 20 short of an all time record. More than that, in the words of John Eastwood and Tony Moyse (in their definitive book 'The Men Who Made The Town') he had 'stuck with the club through the bad times when it often seemed that only he stood between the club and disaster'. Regardless of this, Baxter's fractious relationship with the rookie manager was to create the real crisis point of Robson's tenure at Portman Road.

In January, Baxter put his name to a Sunday paper article about life at Ipswich which was critical of the new regime. These days such a thing would be par for the course as just about every prima donna considers it his right to blab his over paid mouth to the tabloids whenever his ego is wounded regardless of the implications on his club and its supporters.

In the early 70s it had far more impact and Robson felt duty bound to suspend Baxter for a fortnight and to hand the captaincy to Mick Mills – a move that would prove highly significant.

It's hard to imagine how bad the relationship could have been for Baxter to have taken such an action because he must have known that neither his Manager nor his Board would have any truck with it. Both Baxter and team-mate Tommy Carroll had been dropped before – Carroll having walked out after an argument – so when they were seen to pop open the champagne and celebrate an Ipswich defeat, it was clear that the situation simply couldn't be resolved without someone moving on.

Unsurprisingly, neither player was invited back in to the first team fold and when Carroll tore off the team sheet (accounts vary here as some say that, rather than a team sheet, it was a notice restricting access to the post game players bar only to those players who had participated in the game – a fairly pointed statement) from the notice board and stuffed it in Robson's face with the words 'stuff the fucking team', it provoked the explosion that many must have seen coming. Robson openly admits that it was he who threw the first punch though he takes no pride in it. Baxter joined on the side of Carroll and Cyril Lea on the side of Robson in a four-way scuffle that would have alarmed anyone hoping that the team could steer clear of the current problems by pulling together. It certainly didn't look likely.

Robson has said that he viewed the dressing room fight as a turning point for him and for the club. In 1978 he said that 'I had been a player for 15 years and I always considered that I had spent those years underlining that, whatever the circumstances, I could be a sportsman. What it meant was that, in my mid-thirties, I was having to change my personality. Maybe it was at that moment that I learned that, in football, you occasionally have to sacrifice emotional instincts and put steel in your mind'. He believed that he simply couldn't stand down from such a confrontation; he was building something that would have been derailed – and he couldn't afford another management failure.

Happily, the incident seems to have united the players behind Robson and to have therefore effectively sidelined the two miscreants. Despite their value on the field, Robson had decided that 'their days were numbered' because of what happened off of it. True to form, John Cobbold agreed with the decision so that Carroll left for Birmingham and Baxter for Hull. Neither player recreated their consistency for other clubs and their combined 524 appearances for Ipswich became a footnote as they left Portman Road.

That Robson felt he was able to dispense with established players whose behaviour was unacceptable, no doubt had much to do with the quality of the younger players around whom he intended to rebuild. These included Mick Mills, Trevor Whymark and Colin Viljoen.

Mills had been at the club for 3 years having arrived as a 17 year old from Portsmouth and, whilst he had only once managed performances in double figures before Robson arrived, he would go on to make 44 in Robson's first full season.

Though Whymark (who arrived within a few months of Robson himself) made only 26 appearances between 69 and 71 he would become ever-present in 72/73.

Viljoen in particular would prove a key figure in the Robson years up to the greatest day in the club's history at Wembley in 1978 but his establishment at Ipswich was far from straightforward. Of South African descent, he was allocated a work permit in 1966 only on the basis that he play as an amateur for two years before being considered a resident and therefore eligible to turn professional. He therefore spent 2 years as the Cobbold's gardener although just how much landscaping he took part in was not recorded!

Whilst Robson may have seen Viljoen as a key part of the future, the player himself did not – he was one of several on the transfer list although his value at the time was underlined by the fact that his 12 goals in 70/71 made him the club's leading scorer. Charlie Woods, Ron Wigg, Bobby Hunt, Chris Barnard and Steve Stacey all left but Viljoen and Ian Collard, though listed, stayed. There were far fewer arrivals than departures which again underlines the confidence that the Manager had in his younger protégé's although their day was not yet near

A low-key professional signing in 1971 – and one of stark importance for the future – was that of a young 18 year old from Carlisle by the name of Kevin Beattie.

Beattie joined the club as a junior shortly after Robson's arrival. Described by Robson as arriving 'with his arse hanging out his trousers and a shilling in his pocket', the youngster became an Ipswich Town player by way of a curious journey via Liverpool. A natural athlete (at that stage playing as a striker who would later score all 6 in a 6-0 Youth team win) through school and youth teams, Beattie had a successful trial at Liverpool and was invited back to Anfield to sign forms however, when he arrived at Liverpool station to find no one to meet him, his natural shyness and lack of cash precluded him from travelling under his own steam to Anfield to introduce himself. Instead, he used his return ticket to head back home.

John Carruthers – Ipswich's northern scout and a man with an exemplary record of unearthing future stars – was already aware of the lad and quickly jumped in to offer him a trial game with

Ipswich youths against Fulham in London in which Beattie performed outstandingly and was consequently invited to Ipswich to sign. This time there was a welcoming party from Chief Scout Ron Gray (who had looked after him in London for the Fulham game) and from Robson himself. The youngster – short on confidence – had found his family at a club (and town) that he admitted he'd never before heard of. Club and player retain an extraordinary respect for – and gratitude to - each other to this day.

Beattie was joined in the Youth team of the time by Brian Talbot and Roger Osborne – two local lads who were making a name for themselves in what was becoming a very important source of raw material that Robson would mould for the future. Although both players had signed professional forms by 1971, neither would make their first team debut for a few years (Osborne in 1973 and Talbot in 1974) so their preparation and education was in full swing. The Youth set up was in fact established by Jackie Milburn however it was Robson who was quick to recognise it, nurture it and, most importantly, to blood the youngsters at first team level. Considering what was to come, this is a critical element of the Robson story

At first team level, goals were yet again causing a problem. The Clarke/Robertson partnership that was so critical in the previous season delivered just 13 goals even though both players were pretty much ever present throughout the season.

Clive Woods was becoming a regular face – he notched 28 appearances and 1 goal and his skilful and mercurial presence had been the basis of Robson's relatively swift promotion of him to first team duty as Woods signed professional forms just a few months after Robson's arrival. Robson saw in the former junior, a range of skills and trickery (describing Woods as 'cheeky with the ball at his feet') that should have been – and would later be – the source of many more goals.

Defensively things were brighter. Mick Mills – now captain – played 100% of the league programme which added to 35 and 40 respectively in the previous two – Robson had found his rock. Another significant find was a reserve goalkeeper called Laurie Sivell who came in when regular keeper David Best was injured and remained first choice until he himself suffered the same fate. These were rare highlights though in a season that began to stretch the patience of the Portman Road faithful.

The Board remained staunch in its support. The height of its loyalty was reached when it awarded Robson a contract (to replace the verbal 2 year commitment) just as the team hit bottom of the League in 1971! Cobbold famously explained that 'our manager's name is not written in chalk on his door with a sponge nailed by the side'. It was at many other club's and most certainly is now at many more. Again, some might see the Chairman's decision as pig headedness – insisting on keeping his word in spite of the evidence in front of him of the failings of the team under the manager's stewardship. Cobbold though had said all he needed to say about what he thought of Robson when offering him the job – and then he had stood by the Manager when both results and personnel calamities tested his nerve. The word 'admirable' comes nowhere near.

The Board's loyalty was all the more remarkable because of the many lows of the season. One, that was out of anyone's control, was the award of a 'goal' for Alan Hudson's shot in an away defeat at Chelsea which replays clearly proved had hit only the side netting; Chelsea manager Dave Sexton agreed. Robson committed to 'protest to the League in the strongest possible terms' which included a demand that the game be replayed although he probably had little expectation that it would be.

On top of the dressing room woes and abuse from the terraces, this must have felt like another kick in the teeth for Robson and, though he will have been comforted by the loyalty of his Board and Chairman, he wasn't looking for consolations. His own inner drive was keeping him afloat and looking ahead. That was just as well because a final position of 19th and slightly decreased gates over the previous season once again did little to persuade his detractors.

****

Summer was a nightmare for me. Quite apart from hay fever rendering me a snivelling, puffy eyed and incoherent mess, there was no football.

In light of another unspectacular season and the fact that all my school mates were lording it around in their Leeds or Arsenal scarves (the latter had won the League by 1 point but Leeds remained a consistent top 2 side and the kids of Kent who probably couldn't find Yorkshire on the map remained committed), it might have been a good opportunity to leave football behind.

Indeed there were distractions. Our family of 4 was regularly joined by Aunt, Uncle and three cousins in our summer holidays to Swanage in Dorset. This meant an uneven (and frequently fractious) group of 3 girls and 2 boys looking for entertainment on the sandy beaches, in the amusement arcades and Ice Cream parlours of a typical English seaside town. Despite Castles to raid, Tank museums to visit (I don't think that my Mum or Aunt will ever stop dreading the mention of Bovington Tank Museum – a staple of us boys year after year) and war comics to devour, there was always something missing. There are pictures of summer holidays in which I am posing but there are no spades or sandcastles in sight – just a football.

The sun of course was no reason to stop playing the game and the local Rec (I still can't bring myself to call it a Recreation Ground) remained the centre of our universe with the proverbial shirts for goalposts doing us just fine. There remained little competition to my 'being' Jimmy Robertson and, indeed, my choice of affiliation continued to cause a mix of bemusement and amusement which was pretty understandable on the whole.

Nowadays, the close season has a momentum all of its own with the 24/7 stream of news (often just rumour or fiction dressed up as such) via 'always on' media. Back then, the national newspapers were pretty much our only source of information and in the summer months they devoted themselves to the task of updating us on Australian Rules football (an excuse to continue giving punters a reason to play the pools) and cricket neither of which aroused much, if any, interest in me. The summer therefore lay ahead – a barren time with hours to be filled as a chore.

At the age of 9, I certainly wouldn't have appreciated the level of work that must have been going on at Portman Road in those sunny months. Following a poor showing in the League for the first team there was potentially some hope on the horizon through the Reserves and Youths – both of which had finished a creditable 5th in their respective Leagues. I though would have been more interested in where we were going to find a Peter Lorimer or a Charlie George to give me some parity in the playground or – at that point maybe – on the beach.

Turning The Corner

The 1971/1972 season began at a new look Portman Road. Close season work had started on the new Portman Stand (now The Cobbold Stand) that would deliver both an increased capacity of 37,000 and an opportunity to introduce perimeter advertising – a revenue stream previously unrealised on the books. There's no record of the reasoning used to justify the investment for the first of these developments since a 4th from bottom finish the previous season had hardly led to a scramble for season tickets. Equally, there can have been little expectation that the previous season's average of 20,500 would be so comprehensively breached as to require the extra capacity.

In the event, it was a transitional season in which some signs of recovery were clear for all but they were borne out of further trauma and adversity. Equally clear were some signs of Robson's shrewdness and intelligence – it seemed that he was rising above the early problems and was gaining confidence as he built 'his' Ipswich.

He might never have had the opportunity however. George Best played a starring role in Manchester United's 3-1 League Cup win at Portman Road in September 1971. The fact that Ipswich had been undone by probably the best player in the British game at the height of his powers held no sway for the crowd that night who sang 'Robson Out'. When John Cobbold called a Board meeting for the next day, his promise of a minimum two year tenure must have been ringing around Robson's head but he needn't have worried.

Cobbold started the meeting briskly with the words - 'Gentlemen, the first business of the day is to officially record in the Minutes the apologies of this Board to the manager for the behaviour of the fans last night. Agreed? If it ever occurs again at this ground I shall resign as Chairman.' Swift and to the point. It's another of those wonderful Cobbold stories that can be viewed with such romance with the benefit of hindsight. Had Robson not turned the corner, fewer Ipswich fans would probably have been quite so admiring.

The importance of the Chairman and his family over the entire history of the club rings through so many stories. It was sad therefore that Director – and previous Chairman - Alistair Cobbold died thus removing one more link to the historic Cobbold connection. He was (in the words of Tony Moyse and John Eastwood) 'amongst those most responsible for the policy of non interference with the Manager' so his passing could hardly have been more poignant.

Following the Board's vote of confidence, Robson was given the approval to make an acquisition that would prove to be one of the most significant in his creation of the first 'Robson-designed' team. This was the arrival of Allan Hunter, a rugged (the term barely does him justice) central defender from Blackburn spotted by Chief Scout Ron Gray. Making his debut just two days after signing for the club, Hunter went on to complete 35 appearances that first season and was a brick wall that strikers rarely breached. Described by later team-mate Kevin Beattie as 'an absolute legend', Hunter was rarely given the credit that he deserved because his abilities transcended his hard man stopper image – he was calm and organised with the sort of presence that steadied the ship for all around him. Indeed, such was his immediate impact that the performances of his partner Derek Jefferson were apparently recognised as benefiting from his presence – no mean feat given Jefferson's four year tenure in the side.

The promise of the club's Youth Team – built on the foundations of an excellent scouting system led by Ron Gray and also featuring key men including John Carruthers – was recognised by the appointment of Bobby Ferguson as new Coach. Robson's moves into the transfer market remained (Hunter being a particularly key example) but he was ever keener to develop players and to give them their chance at first team level which was an admirable aspect of the club that prevails even to the present day.

The transfer market did however deliver two very significant arrivals – Bryan Hamilton (a former part-timer) from Linfield and Rod Belfitt from Leeds. Going the other way was Frank Brogan to Halifax. Brogan had been a key member of McGarry's Championship winning side but his appearances had decreased under Robson and his departure looked inevitable.

Hamilton was an industrious midfielder whose tenacity was clear from the off. His signing was certainly a risk – a part-timer from a lower standard of football being thrust into the first division at the age of 24 but his performances in a Northern Ireland shirt at the Home Internationals convinced Robson. How right he was – even though Hamilton made just 8 appearances in that first season, he would be ever present the following and has continued an affiliation with the club in various guises including player and coach pretty much ever since.

Belfitt was also a hit from the start – scoring in his first 2 games for the club and finishing the season as equal leading scorer (with Mick Hill) with 7 goals in 26 games. Not the most gainly of characters, his work rate was however undeniable and his finishing was top class – an antidote to the problems that the team had suffered in that area (Jimmy Robertson, for all his flair and creativity, continued to be more provider than finisher in front of goal with just 2 in 40).

The Belfitt/Whymark front partnership seemed to have a little more swagger too. Certainly the Belfitt sideburns became a notable presence to those of us placing posters on our walls.

1971/72 continued to see goalkeeping duties shared between David Best and Laurie Sivell with Mick Mills a constant in the back four and Colin Viljoen equally prominent in midfield. Elsewhere however, the team was changing shape in front of our eyes and the arrivals of Belfitt and Hunter alongside the continuing maturity of Whymark and Mills gave the team a new – if incomplete – look.

Belfitt was key for me. I was able to point out to the Leeds kids in the playground that we had taken a player from them – they of course were always confident that he'd not been good enough to play for the mighty Elland Roaders but our eventual mid-table finish represented an improvement that gave me greater pleasure than their third second place finish on the spin.

This improvement was, to be clear, modest but recognisable. Certainly the players' peers were seeing the change – Crystal Palace's programme notes for Ipswich's visit described Town as 'turning in some classy and intelligent displays for which they have received scant credit'. A finish in 13th was well away from relegation and some notable results (including wins over Manchester City and Spurs) gave us something to cheer about but the season had its fair share of downers too – not least of which was a 0-7 mauling at Bramall Lane, Sheffield. The Blades also played a part in a fiery return game at Portman Road in which Colin Harper was sent off – unjustifiably in the view of most of the home crowd whose anger necessitated a police escort for the official. This was, and is, a rare sight indeed at Portman Road. The significance of the dismissal would turn out to be far greater than was apparent that day in April 1972.

****

If 1971-72 had shown signs of Robson's inspiration then 1972-73 was the start of a period that exemplified his genius. Several individual events signified the fact that we had ourselves an exceptional manager.

The first was the promotion to the first team of Kevin Beattie, now a defender under Robson's tutelage. Robson recognised something special in Beattie from the off and christened him 'The Diamond' (an epithet that, in turn, earned a nickname from his youthful team-mates – 'Bobby's boy') so the chance for a relatively early first team run must have been on the cards. In the event, the move was prompted by the absence of regular left back Colin Harper due to suspension for the Sheffield United sending off. Harper was an experienced and solid full back and would have been hard to replace – he'd been ever present the previous season – so it was not a change that Robson would have taken lightly, 'diamond' or not.

The enforced change though unleashed on the world the most exceptional footballer I have ever seen wear the blue shirt. Robson saw this – along with John Carruthers and Ron Gray – before but it was probably only Robson who recognised the fearlessness of youth combined with the sort of natural power that would equip him for promotion to the first team at a tender age.

So it was Beattie who stepped out at Old Trafford on 12 August

1972 for the season opener – and promptly set up the first of two Ipswich goals in a 2-1 win Beattie's instant admirers included Sir Bobby Charlton – a hero who lined up against the young Cumbrian – and there would be many others. Robson's footballing brain had identified the talent but his man management had gone further. Sensing the fact that the lad wouldn't be overawed by the occasion and would be even further motivated by having his parents watching, Robson had arranged for them to be there (driven down from Carlisle by scout John Carruthers) before even telling Beattie that he was playing. It was the icing on the cake for Beattie. More than that, Robson had boosted the youngster's confidence in the dressing room before the game by telling him that he'd be 'too good' for Willie Morgan (who he'd be marking) and so making the debutant feel 'ten feet tall.'

It's no coincidence that Beattie was one of the apprentices outside the dressing room during the young manager's showdown with Baxter and Carroll and that he had not only respected his manager for making a stand but had wanted to dive in on his side. Whilst we fans would have known nothing of this background, it's critical to the sort of team spirit and togetherness that Robson was building and few players were a more important product of it than Beattie whose warmth and respect for 'The Boss' shine through his every word on the subject

The second was a piece of transfer business that baffled many at the time – including myself as a boy looking to retain his heroes. Rod Belfitt who had been proving a significant solution to our goalscoring problem was sold to Everton (to become Joe Royle's strike partner) after 14 appearances and 6 goals in the new season. Few could have seen the logic – why sell a successful recruit after only 46 appearnaces (barely a season's worth) and in the middle of the sort of form for which the Manager had quite rightly received great credit? Of even greater confusion was the nature of the deal – Belfitt plus cash went to Everton and a 20 year old striker called David Johnson, of whom most knew very little, arrived at Portman Road.

The answer to the conundrum arrived quickly and, once again, showed that Robson was a step ahead. He had recognised that the team would be better balanced by a more conventional and predatory centre forward linking up with Whymark. Johnson had been courted by both Crystal Palace and Liverpool so Robson's success in securing him – and the courageous way that he went about it – spoke volumes.

In 1979, looking back at the landmark moments of his first 10 years at the club, Robson was in no doubt that the signing had been significant not just for what Johnson did for Ipswich but also the mere fact that the club was able to capture him. Robson explained that it was generally difficult to persuade ambitious players to come to what they saw as a 'backwater for a player with ambitions'. Johnson apparently 'took some persuading as did his family. But he came and he played for England as an Ipswich player'.

Ipswich's fearsome front two partnership had been born and would contribute 18 goals that first season – supplemented by another 11 from the blossoming midfielder Bryan Hamilton. Robson's buys were shining.

The changes didn't stop there. Mick McNeill moved to Cambridge and Jimmy Robertson to Stoke. If the absence of our favourite flying winger left us with a style deficit we needn't have worried – the new front pairing more than filled the gap. Robertson's place too was taken by youngster Mick Lambert whose role in the coming years would be constant – if not spectacular – and critical.

One final – and again enforced – change would provide a critical piece of the jigsaw. Following a disciplinary problem, Derek Jefferson moved on to Wolves and Robson moved Beattie into his place in central defence with Harper back to his left back slot. In addition to our Johnson/Whymark partnership, we now had the classic central defensive pairing of Hunter and Beattie or – as Robson christened them – 'bacon and eggs'. Their partnership really was that complementary – the youngster's brash confidence and ball playing skills (he also weighed in with 5 goals that season) sitting alongside the experience and organisation of the Irishman.

There was a sense of reinvention and optimism in the air. Everything felt new. It was therefore appropriate that the team for the first time sported a new club badge designed via a competition organised by the local newspaper. The winning design combined the classic Suffolk Punch horse with evocations of the town's coastal location and ancient history. It updated the rather staid town coat of arms that had preceded it and it represented the town's football club – rather than the town - as a real entity in its own right. The addition of some rather snazzy white collars added to the marked change in kit – a shirt that (complete with new club badge sewn on by my mum) now replaced the rather plain old version worn in all kick abouts by the Kent Town fan. Things were moving on.

For me too things were changing. In 1973, I moved from the small village primary school to secondary school; from a school with probably less than a hundred pupils to one with well over 1000. The Local Education Authority must have had some rather odd logic in mind when they named our institution 'The Wildernesse School For Boys' and for many years later I slightly struggled with the fact that I had been educated in the wilderness(e) although anyone seeing my exam results would have been less surprised.

TURNING THE CORNER

Joining a school with kids from a wider catchment inevitably underlined the differences. For us from a small village there was some talk of yokeldom although I should point out that the school served a relatively narrow area around the leafy suburbs so there weren't too many urbane sophisticates to be found anywhere. Finding a common bond to bridge any gaps was a serious business and, for many, footie affinities would do the job. Not for me though. I never found another Ipswich fan.

The pool of affiliations was not quite as tiny as it is nowadays where kids walking down the high streets from Dartmoor to Dagenham to Durham are likely to be wearing a Chelsea or Man United shirt. Nevertheless, you'd not expect too much variation from the Leeds, Arsenal and Liverpool triumvirate with the temporary allowance for Derby County too.

I was never that worried about being part of the crowd and it can't have been any coincidence that the kids with whom I most remember talking football were supporters of other 'outsider' clubs at the time – Manchester City and Coventry. The latter in particular caused much confusion being as the lad in question was Irish and had just moved to the area from the Midlands where he'd been a regular at Highfield Road (this in itself was odd - someone who actually went to the game every week?). Most kids we knew had about as much knowledge of the Midlands as they did of East Anglia.

I was aware however that things were looking up for my club and that the wider world would be catching on to it. 1972/73 summed up those changes and they ran parallel to a new life for me. I didn't know just how much things were going to be shaken up or just how aware my school friends were going to be of my affinity with this quiet corner of the east – if I had been I'd have maybe taken the time to enjoy it a lot more.

Ipswich was the youngest team in the First Division and we were announcing our arrival. The top 3 clubs that season were Liverpool, Arsenal and Leeds – only the Londoners did the double over us and, on top of the creditable results against these sides, we beat other high fliers including Wolves, West Ham and Derby to finish fourth. That's fourth. European Trips too were now on the cards via qualification for the UEFA Cup.

There were many stars – Beattie, Viljoen (coming into his own as a cultured and many faceted midfielder with vision and poise), Hunter and Johnson amongst them. But there were stars just outside our vision too – the reserves won the SE Counties league by 6 points and the Youths won the FA Youth Cup in a two legged final watched by over 11,000. That Youth team included Robin Turner and John Peddelty who would go on to appear in the first team – alongside George Burley and Eric Gates whose later roles would be very central and Dale Roberts whose association with the club would prove to be long, honourable and multi faceted.

The country was beginning to take notice. 'Match Of The Day' visited 5 times and Anglia's ITV coverage continued with renewed fervour at the achievements of one of its local clubs (debate continues to this day as to which of these clubs enjoys the station's most uncritical support.) MOTD's coverage of the 4-1 home win against Manchester United in front of a record 32,000 crowd must have played a significant part in drawing the football world's attention to the resurgent 'small town' club. Bryan Hamilton's two goals also provided a timely reminder of the manager's ability not only to spot a talent but also to leap in where others pondered.

Robson was pointing out the facts in plain language – in a quote to the Daily Express following a win at St James's Park he said 'when you win at Old Trafford and Newcastle and draw with Leeds you can't be a bad side. For too long we have been looked at as country bumpkins. People had better start to take notice of us'. The Express' Desmond Hacket agreed when he described Ipswich as 'one of the most underrated teams in the country' and his colleague Philip Osborn agreed that Ipswich were 'talented and lively'.

Suddenly we had international players – Mills, Beattie, Whymark and Johnson all earned Under-23 caps for England whilst Hunter and Hamilton continued to star for Northern Ireland. We also had the 'big' clubs sniffing around our stars. Blimey, we had stars.

An early sign of these clubs' arrogance appeared when Manchester United very publicly stated their interest in Mick Mills. Just as happens today, it seems that the biggest clubs feel that they need only mention their interest in a player for both player and current club to immediately succumb to the glory and the cheque book. This situation would become a recurring theme at our club not just through the Robson years but well beyond and to this day. It is the same for many other clubs that invest in a strong youth and scouting policy only for the biggest clubs to consider everyone else as their own nursery. In 2008, it was good to see a number of Chairmen beginning to put pressure on the FA and the League to put an end to the predatory policies of some on youth teams but whether this has any effect or not remains to be seen.

In any event, it won't stop the merry-go-round of established players especially as transfer stories are often sponsored by the tabloids daily quota of gossip and rumour. The only hope for supporters of clubs like Ipswich is that the Board and Manager will stay firm – and that the player will remember who made them attractive to other clubs in the first place.

So often, as supporters, we wonder why players and managers can't say unequivocally that they aren't going anywhere. That's what Mills and Robson said – sort of.

Mills (always a rather introverted character off the field and maybe lacking in the PR charisma too often necessary for punditry and managerial careers) was of immense importance on the field to Ipswich. He was a commanding and exemplary captain around whom Robson knew that the team would be built. In 1972 however he saw a great opportunity at a big club and would have gone were it not for the fact that Robson was unable to find an adequate replacement. Like Robson, who was similarly tempted by some huge names offering him moves away from Portman Road, Mills never regretted the outcome. Four years later he said that he was glad that he stayed put because he'd enjoyed every minute at Ipswich. That sentiment has remained ever since; no regrets, acceptance of the reasons and no tantrums at the time – this was the behaviour of two gentlemen unrecognisable to the prima donnas of the 21st century. So Manchester United were sent packing and Mick Mills continued en route to his all time appearance record.

As an 11 year old watching the side away at Crystal Palace (a club that I might more reasonably have expected to support on geographic grounds), I was excited to see the side take a point but alarmed that David Johnson was injured after only 15 minutes. The result was one of several at this late stage of the season that ensured that there would be no league silverware but they did not detract from the enormous leaps that had been made.

The season did end up with something for the trophy cabinet in the shape of the Texaco Cup – an Anglo Scottish competition comprising 9 English and 7 Scottish teams. Whilst this is not a competition that will be widely recognised or fondly remembered today, it was certainly significant to us for two reasons. Firstly that it was Robson's first trophy and a fitting indication that 72/73 was a key turning point. Secondly that

TURNING THE CORNER

the final had been won over Norwich. Almost 36,000 were at Carrow Road to see Ipswich finish off the 4-2 aggregate win with a second 2-1 result – the winner scored by Norwich born (but Ipswich loved) Clive Woods.

The cup win was the icing on the cake for we supporters who were beginning to believe. Noise at Portman Road was turned up and, as Bobby Robson said in his programme notes in March 1973, the crowd for the Manchester United and Arsenal games created successive attendance records (31,800 and 34,600 respectively). Over the years, there would be plenty of debate over the quality of Town support but Robson was always 100% honest in his appraisal – in this case paying tribute to 'the marvellous support given to the players' who were 'enthralled by the atmosphere'.

The end of a great season was an ideal time to contemplate an event that had taken place right at the beginning of it. In the summer of 1972, in rather quieter surroundings than these bumper crowds, Everton Chairman John Moores approached his Ipswich counterpart to ask for permission to speak to Robson about moving to Goodson Park. Cobbold discussed it with his manager pointing out that 'I expect they'll offer you more than we're paying. How about a ten year contract Bobby?' to which Robson replied 'That'll do me'. By October 1973 Robson revealed to the (London) Evening Standard that 'I've been so busy since then that I haven't had time even to work on the draft of a contract let alone sign one' Priceless.

As we reflected on a fourth place finish and some silverware, I wonder how many of us were aware – or at least aware of the significance – of that meeting the previous summer.

www.cultfigurepublishing.com

ON THE MAP
Life at The Top

1972/73 had either proven that the tide had turned or it was just an aberration. Only time would tell. Well, not very much time actually.

A 24 goal partnership between Johnson and Whymark (not to mention a very impressive contribution of 16 via midfield from Hamilton) propelled Town to a second consecutive fourth place finish and made us the league's top scorers. Although well behind champions Leeds, we were just one point behind Derby who would take over as champions within a year.

The solid core of the team remained but some key new faces appeared. Not least of these was a young right back, a graduate of the successful youth side, called George Burley. Robson recognised in him a natural fitness and timing that was almost unheard of in a 17 year old and acknowledged this with a regular place in the side enabling the young Scotsman to rack up almost half a season's appearances.

Beattie and Mills were ever present throughout the 42 games and, with Hunter making 34 appearances, a familiar looking backline was forming although it still conceded rather too many goals (the 58 'against' column for Ipswich was more than any other side outside of the bottom six).

LIFE AT THE TOP

Another significant new face was in the midfield – Brian Talbot appeared 15 times and contributed 3 goals. This was an early indication of his significance to the club. Over the years, 'Noddy' would be a real hero for the fans who recognised him as being born and bred in Ipswich and – as Robson would later say – having 'a place in his heart for the club'. And what a heart. There can be few midfielders who ever covered more blades of grass with more courage. Robson picked out his 'great stamina, enthusiasm and endurance' all of which shone through but he also had significant creativity to complement his engine room. At that early stage, Robson was still creating 'his' Ipswich and the emergence of Brian Talbot would be a very important part of the process.

Just one season after his arrival in the first team, Kevin Beattie won the PFA Young Player Of The Year as well as being called up for the full England side. Robson's description of him thirty years later – 'a phenomenon' – was being played out for the whole country to see.

Making way for the new faces were Mick Hill, David Best and Frank Clarke all of whom had made important contributions to the club but whose roles going forward were very clearly likely to diminish.

Best's departure in particular was based on a rethink about the goalkeeping position. Over the last three seasons, the spot had been shared between Best and Laurie Sivell (as brave a goalkeeper as anyone will ever see) but Robson had seen someone at Birmingham whom he felt could claim the place as his own. Paul Cooper initially joined on loan but Robson was keen from the off – he recently highlighted the keeper's 'wonderful agility' and pointed out that Cooper was so 'incredibly quick' that he was the 'only one in the squad who could give Beattie a race'. We supporters would see this for ourselves many many times over the years alongside his quiet and critical consistency.

There was too a hugely significant (for some) change in the sartorial department – the stylish button down shirt. In what to me was the most important style statement yet, Town players were resplendent in a new strip that seems now to be quintessentially 70's. For me, the age of the replica shirt had arrived and I could now take on the swaggering open necked style of David Johnson with that bit more authenticity. This was important stuff for an 11 year old and the decision would be noticed because I no longer had to explain to people who Trevor Whymark, David Johnson and Kevin Beattie were. The world was noticing.

For me Whymark in particular was a hero of epic proportions whose ability to head a ball has simply never been bettered. There were no end of finishes from him in which he gains ground on defenders who are odds on favourites - there was something about his athleticism and nose for an opportunity that won him challenges for which he had no right to even compete. The BBC captured one perfect example in a win over Liverpool in which, from a Johnson cross, he practically arches his body around the defender tracking back to squeeze a header into the top right hand corner in probably the only position that the keeper simply couldn't cover. Spectacular though it was, he seemed to do this routinely.

For my dad and I the long trip from Kent was becoming a staple of our weekends. We were both thrilled by this front partnership and we took our place at increasingly earlier times in order to bag a decent spot in the days before booked seat numbers – or indeed seats. The atmosphere had changed to one of expectation but never arrogance. I think that we all knew that Town were punching above our weight. We were now consistently way above 'big' names like Spurs, Arsenal, West Ham and Newcastle and we were enjoying it but never taking it for granted. We also knew that we needed some recognised silverware to make our elevation official.

Recognition by the football world was best illustrated by the return of European football to Suffolk. The first round of the UEFA Cup could hardly have provided a more dramatic indication of progress. A 1-0 aggregate victory over Real Madrid was seen by Robson six years later as the second most important achievement (after the 1978 FA Cup win) of his reign so far. He had a point. In particular, the 0-0 draw in Spain grabbed the headlines. In his own words - 'to go to that magnificent stadium and face 90,000 Spaniards and players like Netzer, Pirri and Amancio was a hell of an experience. The trophy room itself could have brainwashed us into submission. In fact we played superbly, not only defending well but creating the best chances. Even the crowd were on our side in the end and they couldn't pronounce our name before the match. We were on the map.' Mick Mills felt that proactive tactics were the key – the Real manager having admitted that they were expecting a defensive damage limitation approach but in fact faced a side that took the game to them on their own patch. In Mills' opinion (which was shared by the English press) Town could have scored five or six – this was certainly no case of 'hanging on' for a goalless draw.

That extraordinary European curtain opener was no one off. It was followed by a 6-4 aggregate victory over Lazio in which Trevor Whymark scored all four in a first leg 4-0 win at Portman Road. Whymark was such an accomplished player and this was most definitely his night - how often does an Englishman score all four in a European mauling of this magnitude? An odd postscript to the match was revealed by Whymark thirty five years later when he recalled that the tactics for the night had intended to put him in the face of their sweeper in order to free up space for strike partner David Johnson. In the end the opposite happened – Whymark bagged the goals and Johnson unfortunately bagged a serious injury.

The away leg in Rome was closer to a boxing match than a football match. Ipswich's two away goals (from Viljoen and Johnson – the latter neatly avenging the injury inflicted on him quite intentionally by the Lazio defenders in the first game) cemented dominance over the tie. Victory came at a price however. The Italians' tactics may have been hinted at by their game with Arsenal two years earlier that generated kicking and spitting aplenty during the game and a fist fight at a meal afterwards!

On the pitch that night it seemed that Lazio reprised their earlier plan. Robson's instructions to keep calm were tough to follow especially for Hunter and Beattie whose natural inclination was always to protect their own (many a centre half has felt their wrath after dishing out something unsavoury to one of the Town smaller lads). It's highly relevant then to recall the views of Allan Hunter who says that he has 'never witnessed anything remotely as bad.' In Hunter's memory, the antics included head butting a linesman who awarded Town a penalty for a trip on Woods, fans invading the pitch and Lazio players attempting a scissor kick on Whymark.

Any hopes that the final whistle may have bought an end to this were dashed – the normal tradition of handshakes was replaced by burning Union Jacks, Town supporters being attacked and even players being kicked and punched by a mob as they headed for the changing rooms. Once inside, there was little peace as the Lazio players continued to try and kick down the door.

There was some sort of happy ending though; Lazio fans were waiting outside the team's hotel so the police diverted the coach to another one which turned out to be full of rival Roma supporters who partied with the players through the night!

LIFE AT THE TOP

In the third round – by way of total contrast – Dutch side F.C. Twente (who included Frans Thijssen) contributed to two quality games from which Ipswich came out 3-1 aggregate winners (through Whymark, Morris and Hamilton) before bowing out of the competition on penalties in East Germany to Lokomotiv Leipzig. Departure on this basis is always galling (and it wouldn't be the last time that we suffered this way) but the fact that Mick Mills had been contentiously sent off and Brian Talbot had hit the bar in the last few minutes in Leipzig made it even more so. But what a run it had been. Once again, people simply had to take notice.

Robson's tactics (particularly in Madrid) were focused on attack and therefore differed from the more cagey game generally played in European competition. Although these were early days for the manager who would go on to unprecedented club level success across the continent by displaying a mastery of tactics for every occasion, European achievement – allied to the league showing – was yet another reason for other clubs to come calling.

Derby County made an approach after Brian Clough resigned but Robson's explanation (4 years later in 1978) was hugely instructive – 'After what has happened to me I have some regard for loyalty. I have stayed at Ipswich because I firmly believed I was involved in building something exciting for this particular area of the country. I have never lacked backing from my Directors....I have watched the developments of players who were already here when I came and I have been responsible for the promotion of youngsters like Kevin Beattie and George Burley'. This neatly illustrated his influence at the club on the pitch and off of it. It also emphasised his appreciation of both the process and the future potential. He was just getting started.

****

Before a ball was kicked in 1974/75 a hugely significant event occurred. When Don Revie became England manager in July 1974, Leeds came calling on the Cobbolds looking for a replacement. It was rumoured that their offer was three times Robson's current salary but once again the agreement between Robson and the Cobbolds (with or without a contract) stood firm. Quite how public this approach was at the time is hard to recall, but the outcome would shape much of the ensuing years; I think we knew of the growing popularity of our manager and the inevitable consequences of 'bigger' clubs assuming that his ambition would move him to their doors. However, seeing evidence to the contrary was an enormous boost.

Indeed, the imagined humbleness and homeliness of 'little Ipswich' was beginning to grate. We felt that it had to be cast aside once and for all and that 1974/75 might be the year to do it. In many ways it was but not quite in the way that we hoped.

A third place finish (just goal difference separating us from Liverpool in runners up position and 2 points from champions Derby) plus an FA Cup Semi Final and a League Cup Quarter Final wasn't bad going. Whilst less publicly acknowledged outside of Suffolk but of equal importance for the future was the double achieved by the Youths – FA Youth Cup and S. E. Counties League winners (as well as two overseas tournaments thrown in for good measure.) Finally, and maybe perversely, the press seemed to be acknowledging that we were realistic (what nowadays would be called 'professional') challengers – David Miller in the Daily Express observing that 'Robson's team have clearly decided that their challenge for the title demands grinding efficiency rather than blinding spectator appeal'. Complement or insult?

At the same time though, the very same writer waxed lyrical about a 3-0 win over Arsenal that featured 'irresistible' style;

LIFE AT THE TOP

Robson too commented on a performance that was 'the best we've ever played since I came here.' These apparent incongruities simply illustrate that this team was strong in all the areas necessary to challenge. It wasn't possible to be flowing and creative every week – winners could always battle too. Robson would later cite Revie's Leeds side as one of his most admired which is definitive evidence of his appreciation of the warrior qualities necessary alongside the flair. This side had both in spades.

All of these positives were signs of a mature team with a very realistic shot at silverware soon. But when? Ending up with nothing in 1974/75 was galling not least because of the way that we started out of the blocks – 8 wins in the first 9 league games including back to back away wins in North London in our first two games. Between late September and early November though Town couldn't buy a win. Our away form remained too inconsistent throughout although the bid remained on course because of an excellent home record (this phenomenon was to haunt us again over 30 years later and would be equally inexplicable).

Squad strength wasn't the key reason – 8 players made 35+ appearances of the 42 league matches so the team was generally quite settled although these statistics mask the cumulative effect of injuries which, by late in the season, took a significant toll. Once again, Whymark, Johnson and Hamilton contributed 29 goals between them. Our previously somewhat leaky defence was also markedly less porous – actually conceding fewer goals than champions Derby.

It's unrealistic to say that pure bad luck or dodgy refereeing decisions did for us but there are examples of both that certainly didn't help. The key game was the FA Cup Semi Final replay with West Ham at Stamford Bridge in which, by popular consent, Clive Thomas' decisions on at least two occasions cost us a tie that we should have won. The first game had been an epic of attrition in which injuries to Johnson, Beattie and Hunter had meant a constant stream of patching up and positional changes (Whymark played with distinction at centre half which must have been quite a sight as he was never the most robust of players). Ipswich survived and felt that – with improving fitness meaning a return for some key faces – the replay would represent a real opportunity for a first Wembley visit.

It was not to be. Two disallowed goals (one by Hamilton and one by Woods) plus further injuries to Johnson and Hunter scuppered the ambition. It was however the manner of the decisions that cast additional gloom. Robson's comments afterwards were very telling. Clearly emotional, he was also articulate but not as measured as would have been expected then or required today. He said 'There are several FA administrators here and if they don't take action they are failing in their duty to professional soccer and I charge them publicly. I am not asking for the match to be replayed or anything silly like that but if they can sit here, watch this game and be happy then they are letting everybody down. The linesman had signalled a goal when Bryan Hamilton scored. The referee was in no position to give an offside decision'. To neutrals, he seemed to have a point – replays showed that both decisions were, at best, highly questionable but at worst totally wrong. The Daily Express' Steve Curry commented that Ipswich had not received 'any assistance from Glamorgan referee Clive 'The Book' Thomas whose disallowing of two goals was the equivalent of opening up Ipswich's breast and tearing out their heart'. For good measure, Thomas booked six players (three from each side) in what was 'never a violent game'.

Thomas saw it entirely differently. A referee with a reputation for a fondness of his own profile, he was no stranger to controversy and took the opportunity to respond nine years later when writing in his 1984 autobiography 'By the Book'. Thomas' maligning of Robson is worth recording by virtue of the fact that such attacks are rare – maybe unique. Describing Robson as 'one of the few managers in the league that I could not stand', he seemed to take some pleasure in Robson's later dark hours at the helm of England and the root cause of this clearly went back to that 1975 semi at Stamford Bridge. Both Robson and his captain Mick Mills enjoyed near unanimous respect in the game – but not from Thomas who aired similar criticisms of Mills as 'childish' and 'dissentful' whilst an Ipswich player but having improved when he'd moved to Southampton later in his career under a 'manager with a more mature personality.' To complete the set, Thomas had few warm words for the fans too. He complained that refereeing at Portman Road meant that the crowd 'let me know full well what they thought as soon as I ran out on the ground' (this suggests that he may have been tad too sensitive for his role) – acting as 'foolishly as Robson and his players'.

Over thirty years later maybe this whole incident can be consigned to the (still ongoing) debate about the need for independent adjudication or verification of decisions – until we have that, mistakes happen and must be accepted. But these were exceptionally significant. That significance was repeatedly cited as a driving force behind FA Cup success three years later. This strongly suggests that, rather than Robson's actions being foolish or petulant, they were considerably more constructive in turning that anger and feeling of injustice into a determination to put it right. This seems to be the most eloquent retort to Mr Thomas.

Two weeks after the semi-final, the season was over when a draw at Manchester City meant that we couldn't catch Derby. Listening to the heroes of 1978, it is very clear that the heartbreak of the West Ham defeat galvanised them to eventual success three years later but at the time the collapse of the season was a bitter pill for players and supporters alike.

We remained proud of the side. We also sometimes needed to remind ourselves that we were one of the best three teams in the country which neatly summed up how far we'd come. In fact, by any general measure this was an exceptional group of players – Beattie and Johnson making scoring full England appearances alongside Viljoen whilst Burley emerged for Scotland Under 23's and Hunter/Hamilton continued to star for Northern Ireland.

But the big win was no nearer. The season finished with a 4-1 mauling of West Ham at Portman Road (which included the definitive Beattie image of a 40 yard run in which defenders seemed to literally bounce off of him en route to a blast that almost burst the net – sheer raw power) as if to emphasise what might have been. Robson's words in the post match interview probably summarised that 'waiting and hoping' feeling that we all shared – 'if we are patient and we work again next year perhaps it will come our way. We could be, over the next 5 years, a pretty good side.'

The West Ham FA Cup defeat should not have detracted from a great run in the competition in which we previously overcame Wolves, Liverpool, Villa and Leeds. James Lawton wrote in the Daily Express that Mick Mills' 87th minute winner against Liverpool in front of almost 35,000 at Portman Road (with many more locked out after the gates were closed at 2.20) in round four 'ended one of the most compelling cup ties that I've ever seen'. I see his point because it was tense, cheek-by-jowl stuff with little to choose between the sides in terms of style and creativity. This was a tussle in which pure guts pulled us through and it was especially fitting that skipper Mills should claim the winner as he, alongside the rest of the defence, had been totally committed throughout.

The Liverpool result – huge though it was - was to pale in comparison to the quarter final against Leeds that took four games to settle - Clive Woods' glorious winner finally separating the teams 3-2 in the third replay (at neutral Filbert Street) after two 0-0's and a 1-1.

The first Leeds game established the attendance record at Portman Road – 38,010 – that stands to this day (and is unlikely to be broken now that seats have replaced terraces probably for good). The fantastic Town support is best put into perspective when you consider that no less than 15,000 travelled to Leicester for the first replay - Robson commenting on his pride at the support and suggesting (quite realistically at that stage I think) that 'this must have been the biggest away turn out that the club has ever had'. Three years later Robson was still full of pride for a string of performances that 'captured a few hearts' and 'shook the whole country'.

The crush inside Portman Road was the price paid for arrival at the top table. It seems inconceivable these days that getting to the ground by mid day was not an unusual requirement for big games back then. We'd face three hours wait for the kick off, each trying to guard our little claim of land grab only for it to be whisked away as the first surge exploded. Those surges seem a curiosity of history now that we are used to the comfort of civilised seats but back then they were a huge part of the football experience. There was no resisting a wave of human flesh (some of it beer sodden and pretty heavy set too) because the stands had a life of their own when packed and hyped up. Nowadays the involuntary leap for a header that we all seek to suppress from our neighbours are easier to deal with from within our 'personal space' but there was no such thing back then.

After the post Hillsborough Taylor report recommended the abolition of standing areas there was a huge outpouring of nostalgia for the atmosphere that would be lost and much of it was justified but some of the discomfort and tedium of those long waits was lost in the emotion of appeals against it. Especially for a kid, the crowd was a double-edged sword – it was hugely important to the spine tingling excitement of the game (and couldn't be recreated either at smaller grounds or on TV; it was the big match buzz) but it often stood between you and actually seeing the game. Those kids who took their own milk crate to add a few important inches to their visibility may have been complimenting themselves on their (or their parents') foresight but it stood for little as soon as the surge cast aside all in its wake.

All discomforts and inconveniences however ultimately came as a small price to pay for the sheer thrill of taking our place at the top alongside the elite. For me, as a 13-year-old, this was where the Arsenal and Chelsea supporters who'd for so long ridiculed my club would love to be but could only dream about it.

As many names of Ipswich players consequently became increasingly better known, faces continued to change. Paul Cooper quietly joined full-time after his loan spell and going the other way were Peter Morris and John Miller to Norwich, Glenn Keeley to Newcastle and Geoff Hammond to Manchester City. Robson made a very nice net profit from these deals and, in particular, the significance of Cooper's arrival would become clear in the very near future.

Another key personnel moment involved Allan Hunter who had put in a transfer request and was at the point of putting pen to paper on a lucrative move to Leicester before telling himself - 'I just couldn't do it. As I went to sign the contract I began to realise just how much I would miss Ipswich'. He was talking about the town, the quality of life for his family but certainly also the team that Bobby Robson was building. And yet it was Robson himself who prompted the transfer request in the first place. Hunter simply felt that his pay was not in line with his – mainly English – team-mates and wanted parity. Robson ripped up Hunter's transfer requests to him so the defender changed tack by making the request directly to the Chairman which hardly endeared him to Robson. A deal was eventually agreed and Robson's admiration of Hunter has been consistently expressed over the years as testament to their long association. The retention of Hunter was undoubtedly very important. The squad's spirit wasn't being diminished by the heartbreak of near misses – it was being forged and would be key to the coming great achievements.

****

Ladbrokes had Ipswich at 7-1 to win the League at the kick off of 1975/76 and John Morgan in his Daily Express column considered them to have been the best team in the previous season. Portman Road season ticket sales also hit a record high. Not that any of this helped on the pitch as a dismal start left us bottom after three games and it took a decent run in the second half of the season to notch up a top six finish.

The same nucleus of players made up the side but it was also good to see a fair sprinkling of representatives from the successful FA Youth Cup side starting to notch up some performances – Peddelty, Gates, Wark, Bertschin, Tibbot, Roberts and Turner all appearing with the former actually achieving 27 games and 5 goals (often deputising for the injured

Beattie) which would be his best season at the club.

David Johnson's goal return was a very modest 6 from 32 games (largely due to a recurring injury) so the burden really fell on Whymark who responded with 13 from 40 whilst a significant contribution was also made by Mick Lambert with 7 in 30.

Attacking options were limited by the supply from midfield where Viljoen and Talbot both suffered long term injuries and Hamilton – a truly key player – departed to Everton in November. The 54 goal league total was very lean – fortunately the goals against column was similarly modest which attested to a strong defence in which Burley and Mills were 100% ever presents whilst Cooper and Hunter missed just 2 games each.

The departure of Hamilton, like that of Belfitt before him, confused many of us. Though we were now very respectful of Robson's personnel skills, it seemed an odd decision given the Irishman's 4 year tenure during which he made 186 starts and notched 56 goals – a very impressive haul from midfield. More than that, he was the catalyst for much that happened in front of him – always tenacious, intelligent and energetic in distribution and creativity. Robson would have pointed to the very significant profit made by the club on the £40,000 fee and, maybe, also on the emergence of one John Wark who shared with Hamilton a hugely valuable ability to arrive in the box at exactly the right moment to bury a chance. Hamilton's home debut for his new club was a thriller – a 3-3 draw against Ipswich.

My family's trips to Suffolk were now well established. The A12 was not the road it is today and it seems odd that the journey from Kent to Suffolk was consequently quite a major expedition. For weekend games, sometimes my mum would join us (and her sister too) and the womenfolk would head for the shops whilst my dad and I went to the game. Before every High Street and shopping mall had been homogenised out of existence, it was something of a change to visit a different town and my mum must have found it some sort of reward for putting up with the two plus hour journey and the grindingly slow traffic getting in to and out of the town. For evening matches it was just my dad and I and the games were often a more exciting prospect under floodlights but the journey a much longer and less predictable event with school looming after a late night arrival back at home. In those pre mobile days, a stop at a phone box somewhere around Brentwood was a regular posting point for our home ETA (no doubt accompanied by a report on the mood of the boy – i.e. the result!)

I do believe that all of this apparent effort meant something. Over the years I have met no end of fans whose matchday was limited to an hour in the pub before the game and half an hour's journey home afterwards and it's always struck me as attractive. The length of journey has always fundamentally changed the nature of a match – indeed I can't imagine what it must be like to stroll down to Portman Road in my own time. On the plus side, it did however make a major event of pretty much every game (even during some dismal post Robson days when there was nothing much on the pitch to produce such a feeling) and fostered in me an appreciation of my family's efforts - especially my dad's - to satisfy my appetite for the beautiful game.

Despite a modest season – no trophies, early departures in both domestic cup competitions as well as a modest second round in Europe and our lowest League finish for four years - there were some great results along the way. A home win over champions Liverpool was accompanied by a thrilling 3-3 draw at Anfield – not a bad haul against the best. A similar 3-0 win over third placed Manchester United was notable as were two victories over

Dutch giants Feyenoord in the UEFA Cup. The latter in particular were noteworthy not just for cracking goals from Woods and Whymark alongside an inspirational performance by Cooper but also for Robson's tactics - containing the Dutch side and allowing them possession in areas of no threat before breaking away with three or four players in support which left Feyenoord, in Robson's words, 'totally confused'.

Overall however, consistency was sadly lacking and costly – throwing away a 3-0 lead from the home tie against Bruges by losing 0-4 in Belgium was a dramatic example. The final game neatly summed it up in a 2-6 mauling by Derby in which Francis Lee helped himself to two goals on his final appearance before retirement. I'd like to have heard Robson's dressing room discussion of that performance. Even though it was over 30 years ago I remember it very vividly as being a comedy performance against a team that – though finishing fourth – really had little spectacular to offer. It was suggested that Town defenders allowed 'little Frannie' to help himself to a goal or two as recognition of his distinguished career especially as the result would not have affected our sixth place finish but I hope that that wasn't the case – finishing a season with a defeat like that is hardly the way that we fans wanted to head off towards the summer.

Two days after the Derby debacle, Mick Mills' testimonial game was held at Portman Road. In retrospect it seemed a curiously early one. Despite the fact that he had been at the club for ten years at that stage, he had plenty of unfinished business and in fact was enjoying a revitalised career at England level alongside the sort of consistency at Ipswich that we all (very unfairly) took for granted. It is however worth noting Robson's comments – valuable as they are in not only reflecting his admiration for Mills' contribution to date but also in explaining just why his captain would remain at the helm through the greatest years in his reign which were just around the corner.

In his programme notes, Robson said that he had considered Mills to be 'something special' when he originally appointed him as captain and that, ever since, Mills had proved himself the 'ideal choice'. The word consistent was used throughout (Robson saying that he could 'hardly ever remember Mick Mills turning in a below average display') but Robson also stressed the respect felt for him by his team mates, his bravery, organisational skills and personal pride ('he presents an ideal image of the modern day footballer.') Robson was not alone in his admiration of Mills – the plaudits came thick and fast from a range of Managers including Bill Shankly ('you are my kind of player'), Don Revie, Bertie Mee and even Norwich manager John Bond.

Robson said that 'only by the high standards we had set the previous year, could the 1975/76 campaign be judged a failure'. Maybe but possibly Robson had in mind a number of positives of which supporters – focused as they are on the first team – were less aware.

In those days the balance sheet results were not publicised the way they are today. Had they been so then we would have acknowledged a record profit (the princely sum of £165,000!) Not buying any players will have made quite a contribution to this – Robson was planning to mine the rich seam of talent from the Youth side and John Wark's award as Young Player of The Year would have been a highly significant sign of the times in this regard. Another positive was the Reserves successful season in the Football Combination which culminated in winning the title – an achievement to which the young Wark made more than his fair share of contribution having graduated from the youths. That promising source of new talent was on to another batch (which included Alan Brazil and Russell Osman) even then - the Youths also had a championship winning season (under the tutelage of Charlie Woods) in the S. E. Counties League and went a step further by also winning the S. E. Counties League Cup as well.

We knew that these developments were important and we took some pleasure in lifting trophies. But sometimes they didn't feel like real trophies – real pleasures. The fact was that we were indisputably one of the top six sides in English football but, at times, that sometimes felt not quite enough. To some, we had stalled or maybe even taken a small step backward. We hoped that it was a temporary hiccup in the steady trajectory established by Robson; if only we'd known that we had little or nothing to worry about.

****

Regardless of the return achieved in 1975/76, we all agreed that we had the basis of a great side. This was bought into sharper focus shortly before the new season kicked off when David Johnson departed for Liverpool.

Like the previous departures of Belfitt and Hamilton, many of us were left scratching our head at Robson's thinking. Losing one half of the best striking duo that we had had for some time didn't seem entirely logical if we were to start grabbing some silverware. Admittedly, Johnson's return for the previous season had been modest - largely because of injury - and the £200,000 price tag was a very attractive return on investment but the fact remained that we could see no obvious replacement on the horizon from within the club. We trusted that Robson had something up his sleeve; time would prove the move to be simply one of his greatest coups.

Off the field, that summer of 1976 also bought about a change at the top but you'd have been forgiven for not noticing. Patrick Cobbold took over as Chairman from his brother John but the

Boardroom continued with business as usual; everyone was happy with that.

The Express put Town at 16/1 for the title – down from the previous year because they saw the side as 'lacking conviction' despite the obvious talent. A mixed bag of results alongside some significant changes in personnel and positions at the start of the season might have been taken as a sign of transition. A win and two draws from the first three games was followed by a pasting (2-5) at Villa where, despite the result, Manager Ron Saunders said that 'Ipswich were the best side that we've come up against this season'. Young John Wark was moved into midfield (after impressing there in the reserves despite the fact that his few first team games had been in defence) replacing another youngster in Eric Gates who was injured.

Johnson's place had been taken by yet another youngster in Keith Bertschin who had started well with a goal against Spurs in the opener but no one really expected him to fill Johnson's boots just yet. Robson had in mind someone else for that role but he had a battle on his hands.

Paul Mariner was the 23 year old centre forward who would ultimately make the number 9 shirt his own but the deal that took him to Ipswich was protracted and part of a tug-of-war involving West Ham and WBA both of which made offers to his club Plymouth Argyle.

What few of us could have known at the time was that Mariner would have chosen Ipswich even before Robson was in the frame. Having top scored for Argyle in 1975/76 and then started on fire with 8 in the first 10 games of 1976/77, Mariner was being noticed far and wide. West Ham were the first club to make an offer but Mariner later said that 'if I'd had my choice it would have been Ipswich so you can imagine how I felt when the boss phoned back later and said Bobby Robson had also made an offer; when I heard Ipswich wanted me I felt like packing my bags there and then'. He rejected West Ham but Ipswich and Plymouth were mired in talks because Ipswich were offering cash plus player but Plymouth were looking for a cash only deal. When WBA made a cash offer it looked all over. However, somehow the negotiations bore fruit and Mariner became a Town player (John Peddelty and Terry Austin going the other way in what was a record deal for Town). 'I knew that I had joined a club that was going places' he said and he wasn't alone.

At the time I felt it a real coup that we could beat both West Ham and West Brom as both would traditionally have been a bigger pull for a player in demand; it was significant to me that we had got him but I was unaware at that stage of just how keen he had been to join – or just how much he saw of the future of our club. Mariner's enthusiasm was based not only on results and seeing the side play but also the opinions of many others in the game. He later explained that 'Ipswich have a tremendous reputation among other players and the general impression I had was that they were a great club.'

Robson's capture of Mariner – and the mutual respect that they had from day one – was another example of great management. Spotting a player with a hunger to 'step up' is a skill that few have – and it is becoming even rarer. Nowadays, as Agents and players chase multi million deals that include image rights and sponsorship – plus there's some small print somewhere about actually playing the game – managers and coaches seem increasingly less willing to look at the lower leagues for the sort of talent and hunger that makes for great players.

In 2008 we at Portman Road were once again able to point to a player who exemplifies what happens when this type of deal goes right – Jon Walters joined from Chester and has simply been outstanding not just in terms of his playing but his contribution, commitment and attitude; he is often the heart of the side. I am convinced that, both in 1976 and in 2007, the player's view of the move as a step up has been key and that seeking a similar level of commitment and hunger from a player dropping down very rarely bears fruit.

Back then, Robson had known the importance of replacing Johnson - maybe it would be that final piece of the jigsaw – and he had seen something special in Mariner. Most of us at Portman Road on 6th November 1976 saw it too.

A 7-0 hammering of WBA was great enough but there were real extra bonuses. Not only did it include a text book thunderbolt from Beattie and no less than four from Whymark (including one based on a superb one-two with Mariner) but it also signalled the arrival of Mariner. His goal was pure class – picking up the ball just inside the Albion half and running by two or three defenders before unleashing an unstoppable shot form 25 yards. More importantly for us on the terraces, so was his celebration. He ran behind the goal, looked up at the North Stand, put both hands to his mouth and blew kisses to the lot. A star was born. We knew that not only did we have a great new striker but we had someone with some showbiz pizzazz too. Strange to relate that Mariner himself was apparently a very quiet and almost introspective character back then – his success with Town and England would only later bring out the extrovert in him. He later said that 'the fans were terrific and scoring in my first game in front of them was out of this world. I was in a daze for a while after the match'. He wasn't alone. I can remember it like it was yesterday.

If the afternoon highlighted our coup it would similarly have left Albion feeling somewhat bruised at losing the battle.

Mariner would do the same to West Ham later in the season when he netted a hat-trick in a 4-1 Town win. Robson has always considered Mariner to be one of his most important signings and we were just at the beginning of a long association that would prove it to all and sundry.

A spate of injuries (not least to Beattie – a trend that would reduce his contribution in the short term and end his career in the longer term) put paid to the stable line up that had been enjoyed in the first half of the season and, in effect, resulted in a third place finish when many felt that we deserved better.

Champions Liverpool finished just 5 points ahead and we'd been in a storming position until literally the last five or six games when injuries took their toll. There was nothing to be ashamed of in finishing third as was shown by the club record average gate of 26,700. The reserves' season – whilst not quite living up to the previous title – was also positive especially because of the side's huge goal haul (86 in their last 30 games) and the contribution to it of one Alan Brazil as well as Russell Osman's award of the Young Player Of The Year title.

Throughout the season the side won friends and admirers for its style of football. Lest we were getting blasé about it – maybe the same might have been said for how we felt about our manager – it was good to hear others remind us of how fortunate we were. Bill Elliot in the Daily Express described Town as 'a team without weakness'. Everton's caretaker Manager Steve Burtenshaw commented after seeing his side beaten 2-0 at Portman Road – 'I think that most teams facing Ipswich today would have come away being beaten by five or six. They are the best side that I've seen this season. They are excellent. With Ipswich in that form there wasn't a lot you can do to stem the onslaught'. Players were singled out too – David Miller in the Express describing Brian Talbot as the 'most dynamic 90 minute player in the league'.

At the heart of much of the style and many of the goals was the relationship between Mariner and Whymark which – quite literally – seemed to have been cemented instantaneously. Mariner's comment on Whymark after the WBA game (only his second in a blue shirt) summed it up - 'He's a dream to play with. We've found this immediate understanding. Why he's not in the England squad I'll never know'. Many of us struggled with that conundrum.

Once again however, despite the plaudits, the season ended without trophies. Whilst a top three finish, a demonstrable improvement on the previous season and the arrival of a new hero all seemed to bode well for the near future, Robson himself was beginning to betray his own frustration. After a defeat at Middlesbrough in April that all but ended the chance of the title, he told Malcolm Foley – 'I thought that we were good enough to win the Championship. I really did' but he conceded that 'now we've got to qualify for Europe at least and then begin all over again next year.'

I don't recall any moaning that we should by now have been winning trophies – the sort of impatience expressed nowadays with the increased glare of publicity and the ease with which everyone can have their public say. The Robson revolution was in full swing; most of us remembered where we'd come from so we appreciated the progress and lived in hope that the returns would be around the corner. The sheer pleasure of walking side by side with the top teams was to be enjoyed and if we had any sense of disappointment we kept it to the back of our mind and focused on the strides that had been made.

There could be few clubs in the country whose supporters had more right to feel good about the future.

ON THE MAP

A Glorious Blip

Kevin Beattie has said that 1977/78 would have been a washout had it not been for the FA Cup and you can see his point. Robson's rebuilding of the club had been steadily progressing, each season seeing us in the top 6 and jostling for the highest echelons by developing new talent and stretching comparatively meagre resources to the limit. The silverware hadn't arrived but we felt that things were on course. We had almost become accustomed to our place at the top. Finishing 18th then (and, until fairly late on, being in the relegation mix) would have been an unparalleled disaster had it not been for the glorious consolation of Wembley on May 6 1978.

Much has been written about the fact that Robson never won the Championship with Ipswich and the reason is commonly cited as lack of a large enough quality squad to cope with an avalanche of injuries. This did for our championship ambitions several times and 1977/78 was certainly one of them. How else could this odd season be explained when sandwiched between third and sixth finishes either side? The player statistics also tell the story. Not a single player was ever present throughout the 42 league games – only Talbot and Cooper coming close (at 40) with 5 players in the 30's and some very notable names making just a handful – Whymark 19, Wark 18 and Beattie 14. Mick Lambert did not start a single league game.

League results reflected the disruption to the team's rhythm despite a 1-0 win in the first game of the season at home to Arsenal. I recall this as one of the oddest games I've seen in that the rain came down so heavily that the referee called a temporary halt to the game – removing the players from the pitch when the ball was seen to stop dead in its tracks in puddles. Normal service was however later resumed and a goal from young David Geddis – a new face who would become significant during that season – sent us all home happy and with no reason to doubt that we would once again be challenging.

Only three wins in the next 12 rather changed the picture. Goal scoring was a problem - Mariner and Whymark managed 20 between them of relatively meagre 47 in total – but a leaky defence that conceded 61 was at least as significant. This could be seen as the price paid for the break up of the classic four man defence (Burley, Beattie, Hunter and Mills).

Oddly – quite apart from FA Cup glory – amidst all of the league gloom was some temporary good news via another cup competition in Europe. After dispatching Landskrona Bois and Las Palmas in the UEFA Cup, Town took on Barcelona (Cruyff et al) at Portman Road and turned in a brilliant performance to run out 3-0 winners with goals from Gates, Whymark and Talbot. The performance featured an increasingly rare appearance by Beattie just over three weeks after having a cartilage removed.

With such a commanding lead to take back to Spain in early December, everyone must have been confident that not only would we go through but that this might kick start the season. Wrong. I still clearly remember listening to the radio commentary on headphones and attracting the wrath of my dad as my anguished yells in response to Woods' miss in the penalty decider (after a 0-3 defeat) made my parents leap out of their skins (it's so hard to imagine when you're in that sort of cocoon that other people are oblivious to the drama). Hitting the woodwork and having a goal disallowed didn't help and Cruyff himself admitted that Town had been unlucky. Such sentiments however don't change the result or the sinking feeling. Curiously this result – clutching defeat from the jaws of victory – was in spite of a good luck telegram that read - 'Remember Bruges – don't let it happen again'. A nice sentiment especially as it came from FC Bruges.

So 1978 dawned and there had been little to be remembered of 1977 since August. We hoped for better things but cannot realistically have seen them starting at Ninian Park Cardiff on January 7th. To the players though Robson apparently dubbed it the most important game of the season – he was aware that an early exit might leave them with little to play for even at that absurdly early stage. Two Mariner goals in a 2-0 win got us past the third round of the FA Cup but the win was sandwiched between two league defeats (to Arsenal and Manchester United) that would have registered far more as a measure of the continuing gloom.

Later in January a 4-1 victory over Hartlepool (second bottom of the Football League at the time although winners over Crystal Palace in the third round) saw Town into the fifth round. Again though, it was sandwiched between league defeats including one in which we conceded five at Chelsea.

Inevitably there were some supporters who were unhappy. Over the years, Robson never shied away from looking these people in the eye. In the early years when things were at their worst for him he was buoyed by the support of the Board but never complacent that such support would protect him from the views of the fans. In fact I admired him when he went on the offensive which he did many times over the years. In 1977/78 the poor league form created one such example in which he chose his words carefully to be appropriately targeted when he said 'it is obvious that we, like most other clubs, have our fickle supporters with short memories. They have tried to fill my postbag following last week's 5-3 defeat at Chelsea but I have also received some great letters from some great supporters and it is for them that we will try to get things right. Do I really have to remind you that it is at a time like this, when we are being deserted by good fortune and the breaks are going against us, that we need your support more than ever?' I suspect that most of us had little problem with the answer to that question.

One glimmer of hope arising from the enforced changes in personnel was the emergence of Eric Gates. Often associated with the great team of 81, it's easy to forget that he had been at the club since 1972 and had graduated through the youths to start to pick up some first team games over the previous two seasons but his 23 league appearances (and 2 goals) in 1977/78 represented by far his longest run and was a precursor to his becoming an established and hugely influential player form the late 70s through to the mid 80s.

It might not have been so. Understandably, Gates was becoming frustrated at not yet having made the breakthrough (despite some great performances and high profile goals – a cracker against Bruges in the UEFA Cup in 1975/76 for example) and had put in a transfer request which was rejected by Robson on the basis that he saw Gates as a big part of his plans. The question for Gates was when? One thing is for sure – Gates wouldn't have chosen to go. He said at the time – 'I'm always hearing that this club and that are interested in me but if I could fight my way into the Ipswich side on a regular basis I'd forget all thoughts about leaving. After all, when I came to Portman Road in 1972 it was a long journey from my home near Middlesbrough. That's how much I wanted to join Ipswich then and I'm every bit as enthusiastic now.' This passion for the club has obvious parallels with the views of Paul Mariner when he arrived the year before and says a lot about players' appreciation of Robson's way of playing and his policy of giving youth and less fashionable names a chance to shine. For us supporters, the silver lining to the injury of John Wark in 1977/78 was that it gave Gates a chance – we would see the benefits in the not too distant future.

It's pretty much universally accepted that all cup winners have one game in the run in which they ride their luck. For Ipswich in 1978 it was away to Bristol Rovers in the fifth round. On a pitch that many thought unplayable (and more suited as an ice rink), Town were four minutes away from exiting the competition when Robin Turner scored the second of his two goals to rescue the tie at 2-2. It might have been too little too late had Bobby Gould's earlier effort not been disallowed for a dubious offside – had that given Rovers a 3-1 lead the season may have been over amongst the snow of Eastville. Instead, Town comfortably won the replay 3-0 and found themselves in the quarter finals. The importance of the away leg Rovers result seems fitting testament to Robin Turner whose 9 years at Town yielded just 22 first team starts and 50 first team appearances in all; he started 5 of the 6 games in the cup run of that year though and is justifiably therefore considered very much one of the 'class of 78'.

A league win and a draw in the 2 games following the Rovers replay gave us a little bit of consistency to enjoy. Most minds however were on March 11 at The Den where we would take on Millwall in the quarter final. Living in Kent made this an easy journey for me but getting a ticket in the Town end wasn't an option and going in with the Millwall seemed a very unattractive one. Back then their reputation was well known (and, amongst some of them, both enjoyed and deserved). I remember talking about my concerns to our schoolboy team's coach who felt that such fears were unfounded and described the Den as being like a 'Vicar's tea party'. All I can say is that he must have known some riotous clergy because what later went off was no laughing matter.

Nowadays there seems to be an odd nostalgia surrounding football violence of the 70s (one reviewer has dubbed the genre of books on the subject as 'hooligan porn') which is maybe just an example of rose coloured specs now that the experience of going to a game is largely civilised. Ipswich has never had a significant problem of its own (notwithstanding the potential at derby games which are now so oddly scheduled and heavily policed that potential is pretty much all it generally is) although of course the club had its share of participants back then. Moreover, the club and town had to accommodate other people's problems. The closest I ever came to being involved was against Manchester City when a mate of mine – a City supporter – came to Portman Road with me and we were confronted by three or four lads in an alleyway who intended to 'do' him because of his City scarf. They decided against it when I stood with him and the odds looked less positive for them. It was slightly ironic that I might have been battered by our own 'supporters'.

One possible reason for Portman Road being a relatively safe place even during the worst of the idiocy was the fact that Suffolk police in the 80s were gloriously un-PC (as in correct rather than constable) and were not known for their tolerance. I remember Newcastle coming to town and gangs of their number running riot through the town centre sending families scurrying for cover who had nothing whatsoever to do with football violence or even football. Brave lads. As they ran through the shopping area, a police van came to a grinding (and

www.cultfigurepublishing.com

noisy) halt, police jumped out, opened the back doors, picked up a couple of these lads and threw them in the back. I heard the sound of head hitting metal; nowadays you'd hear the sound of Lawyer hitting mobile. The recollection of all this brings to mind just how far we have come since the tragedies of Heysel and Hillsborough bought the whole thing to a head and the match experience changed forever. The fact that the causes weren't necessarily hooliganism didn't change the response which was based on an assumption that they were. So many innocent people tragically died at Hillsborough because the police apparently put two and two together and got it wrong.

There was a period in the 70s when certain fixtures simply meant trouble. They certainly weren't every week – and they were rarely home games - but Millwall away was one of them. And yet, even armed with that knowledge, what happened that day was still a shock to most people. Indiscriminate rioting left women and children with blood stained faces, coaches with smashed windows and the players removed from the pitch for nearly 20 minutes whilst order was restored.

Off the record, Robson had said that the rioters should have the flamethrowers turned on them; he was surprised to hear his words repeated on 'Match Of The Day' very much on the record. His response was typically honest and forthright – saying that 'My after match comments were not meant for public consumption but it has been obvious from the letters that I have received that they summed up the feelings of all genuine football lovers, there have been apologetic letters from genuine Millwall fans ashamed of what happened'.

The press agreed and actually often went further. James Mossop in the Sunday Express wrote 'when the football authorities come to consider the evidence, they will surely decide that Millwall's ground should be shut for a record length of time ' and that

Millwall 'must be ordered to erect fences if the message is to be finally and clearly rammed home to the criminal lunatics who masquerade as supporters.'

It is sad that the behaviour of the crowd should overshadow what happened on the pitch – which was that Town turned on a 'masterful' performance (in the words of Mossop) to run out 6-1 winners and book their place in the semi finals. For the record, Burley and Wark both scored stunning goals whilst Mariner grabbed a hat-trick and Talbot completed the scoring. It was tribute to the players that the off field events did not interrupt their momentum (in fact it seems likely that it did more harm to the home side's concentration) in recording an impressive and emphatic victory.

League form after the quarter final victory unfortunately continued largely unaffected save for a glorious 4-0 trouncing of Norwich just a week before the semi-final on April 4th at Highbury against WBA.

For the players it seems that their biggest motivation for the semi lay not just in the opportunity to salvage some glory from an insipid season but also to wipe away the memory of the club's only other semi-final experience – in 1975. George Burley recently emphasised that 'Highbury meant as much as it did to so many of the players because they had the memory of what happened three years earlier at the back of their minds'. It's so often emphasised that players may only get one chance at a cup final so the fact that the Town team was so young and stable in 75 paid dividends three years later when they had their second chance.

Albion were a quality side. They would finish that season in sixth place having taken three of the four available points from Town in two league games. Their squad included Derek Statham, John Wile, Aly Robertson, Ally Brown, Cyrille Regis (who had scored in each round en route to the semi), Willie Johnston, Laurie Cunningham and a young emerging midfielder called Bryan Robson. They had negotiated a couple of particularly tricky ties at Manchester United and Derby as well as disposing of Blackpool and Fulham before meeting Town at Highbury. Ron Atkinson was the Manager but he was the third occupant of the seat since the end of the previous season (when Johnny Giles left) and so was relatively new in but he had inherited a strong side and Robson knew that this would be a tough game. Town were considered underdogs not only because of their poor league position but probably because their road to the semi had been nothing like as difficult as their opponents' in terms of the strength of opposition.

For Robson of course it was a very significant pairing – against the club that he'd served so successfully as a player. Everything was teed up for a right royal battle. Even the choice of Clive Thomas as referee couldn't have dented the Town players' motivation – indeed their determination to expunge the memory of 75 was almost certainly given greater focus by the fact.

This was the big time. I clearly remember the corridor that ran from the turnstiles underneath the terraces and up into the stand. Such was the sheer weight of numbers that my feet didn't touch the ground from one end to the other and I emerged on the terraces gasping - mostly out of excitement. My Dad had managed to keep his feet – some measure I guess of just how spindly a beanpole teenager I must have been. Once in the ground we were part of a vast wall of blue and a crescendo of noise. If Town were the rank outsiders the news hadn't got through to us.

The starting 11 had a far more familiar look about it. The four man defence was restored – Beattie making one of only twenty one appearances that season – and really only Robin Turner partnering Mariner could be considered outside of a first choice (although Turner had of course done more than his fair share to help Town to this stage.)

It would be foolish to try and describe the 90 minutes but there were some key moments that probably sum it up. The first was after just 8 minutes when Brian Talbot guided a glorious header in to give us the lead but, in so doing, violently clashed heads with John Wile; Talbot departed whilst Wile remained blood stained and bandaged. We had gained the lead but lost a crucial driver of the side.

Twelve minutes later Mick Mills made it two and suddenly we wondered if we could relax – no, that was crazy talk so early and with Town's history of living on the edge. Even so, with things staying that way until less than 15 minutes from the end much of the game was looking controlled and we might even have been thinking about counting down the minutes. Then a hugely uncharacteristic error by Allan Hunter – a hand ball that seemed to be out of pure panic, something unknown to the big man – and a converted penalty by Tony Brown. Normal panicky service is resumed.

The key moments were then. Over the years (both before and many times since) there's been a sort of timid or brittle nature to our confidence when in positive situations. That takes its toll. In a 13 minute period at Highbury that day the nervousness of Suffolk showed itself by a collective silence and stillness. The 26,000-strong wall of blue was there but it was quiet and palpably immobile. People tried to start songs but little took root. Were we counting down the seconds or simply so terrified that we had to look away? The ghost of 1975? The self doubt of almost 10 years of Bobby Robson's admirable development work having not yet generated a recognised trophy? Whatever the reason, it was a long thirteen minutes even though WBA were reduced to ten men by the dismissal of Mick Martin five minutes from time which should have made us more settled. It didn't.

Over the years there have been no end of reasons to admire John Wark. Paul Mariner recently rightly described him as 'an unbelievable player and a great ambassador for the club' - this is true right through to this day; Bobby Robson said that Wark will 'go down in history, rightfully, as one of the greats of our time.' Mick Mills however picked out one moment for which he will always remember Wark and that was Wark's 89th minute header that made it 3-1. Bang on. As soon as the ball hit the net the timidity, the brittleness and questioning disappeared to be washed away in a tide of joy. It was done – there was no more time for doubts or fears.

Amidst the noise and euphoria of us travelling supporters and players was a lovely recollection recorded by Robson. The manager shared that glorious moment with John and Patrick Cobbold of whom he said - 'think what it meant to them? Their father had started the club for heaven's sake and Wembley was just a dream'. There is no better description of just how far the club had come. But Robson wasn't finished and he made this clear when he said that 'the club is populated by some of the nicest people in the game and it will be a wonderful and deserved bonus if we can win the cup for them'.

****

A return to league business bought everyone down to earth. In fact, between that glorious day at Highbury and the end of the season, Town managed just one league victory and that probably secured Davison One status. This is really extraordinary although the fact that Talbot, Hunter and Mariner were all absent from the very next game probably sums up the selection problems that Robson faced all season.

In reality it must have been hard for all of the players' thoughts not to stray from the forthcoming trip to Wembley. In any event, preparation for the final was anything but smooth.

Firstly there was the 'Viljoen affair'. The South African's appearances had been sparse throughout the season but Robson was very much aware of his vision and skill which might be a very important balance against the Arsenal middle of the park in which Liam Brady was so influential. On the other hand Roger Osborne had made twice as many appearances and had been effective as well as flexible – he was what we nowadays (often unflatteringly) call a utility man. Robson had a key decision to make.

In the last game before the final, Robson put Viljoen into the side at the expense of Osborne away at Villa and what happened has become legend - Town were hammered 1-6. The 'myth' which will probably never be properly laid to rest is that the team's abject performance was a statement of their disapproval of the omission of Osborne in favour of Viljoen. Despite much being said and written by the protagonists of the day it's still not clear exactly what happened. Talbot was one of the players who did admit to making his feelings known to Robson about the decision but the suggestion that the players wouldn't accept the same selection for the final (the 'player power' argument) has been roundly rejected by pretty much everyone and certainly by Robson.

A sad footnote to the saga was that it created another victim – Paul Overton was the young keeper that day drafted in because of injuries to both Cooper and Sivell and making his one and only appearance. It was particularly painful for him as his position was one that most supporters would relate to. He said

'I've been a Town supporter for years and I used to travel from Ely for all the games. All I've ever wanted was to play for Ipswich'. It was good then that Robson publicly absolved him of all blame and that Allan Hunter too says that the rest of the team let Overton down 'in a big way.' He had just been in the wrong place at the wrong time.

The second piece of preparation that backfired was a trip to Wembley on the Tuesday before the final. The intention n had been to try out the pitch but it was waterlogged. Then the day before, at the team hotel in St Albans, a practice match had to be called off because the pitch had just been mowed and all of the (previously) long grass was left in place rather than being cleared

On top of this were the injury problems that had haunted the club all season – in particular those to both Beattie and Hunter which were so key to the defence. Whilst Russell Osman had graduated from the reserves to complete an amazing 28 appearances (from a standing start) as a deputy, most felt that the appearance of at least one of these two giants would be of critical importance. Hunter's injury was considered the more serious of the two (Beattie by now, as a matter of near routine, being patched up and pumped full of cortisone to get him though games) so when he passed a morning fitness test some of the negativity that may have been in the air was lifted.

Not that it seemed to have been an issue. Listening to the players talk about it these days, they were never in any doubt that they could – and would – win. Some of this was based on gut feel (Cyril Lea had said that he was certain that the club would win silverware in his 13th season at the club – and this was it) whilst other examples were down to a belief that they were simply better than Arsenal. Take Kevin Beattie as an example who recently said that 'we played brilliantly to beat Albion [in the semi] and there was no lack of confidence about facing Arsenal in the final. Right there and then, as we celebrated getting to Wembley, we fancied our chances and that feeling never really went away'.

Come the day and that confidence had to be proven by a performance. And wasn't it? With the luxury of retrospect it's easy to look at the fiftieth Wembley Cup Final as representing a glorious 1-0 walkover and certainly there have been few such one sided cup finals ever. Looking at it now it may seem inevitable that all of that superiority on the day would eventually spawn a goal but this is Ipswich Town that we are talking about – a club whose performances over the previous years had earned it respect, plaudits, awards and absolutely no major silverware. What's more this is Arsenal we are talking about too – that 'Lucky Arsenal' tag was embedded in everyone's mind the longer the game progressed without an advantage. These doubts are easy to write about now but there was little as considered or level headed going on back then – especially for me.

It may seem inexplicable in these days of hi tech home entertainment for all, but we had no colour TV back then. I was consequently accommodated by my Aunt, Uncle and cousins (and their telly) for the biggest game of my life thereby escaping a monochrome experience of a colourful day. My uncle and cousins were footie mad but as neutrals; they played and watched but had no affinities. It was this that created the tension. They gasped incredulously as we managed to hit the woodwork no less than three times ('would you believe it – they're never going to score') accompanied by raucous laughs as the tangle in my gut became ever more immovable.

It's impossible to describe the chasm of difference between a committed fan and a neutral in a situation like this – I was kicking and heading every ball, my heart pounding and the fear of missing out yet again stalking me through every minute. They were aghast at the imbalance of the game and the likelihood that a failure to make the most of all that dominance would only end one way. I'm sure that I tried to be polite and to keep my anguish to myself; equally I'm pretty sure that I failed.

I remember literally hitting the ceiling when Roger Osborne's shot hit the net. A sense of relief accompanied by a gripping fear that 12 minutes remained to hang on.

The rest of the game would not feature the hero of the hour. Osborne's physical and emotional exhaustion resulted in him leaving the game. In his place came Mick Lambert, almost a like-for-like swap in terms of temperament and profile (although the fact that Lambert holds the record as the only footballer ever to play in a cup final and also be picked in an England cricket team ought to be stressed on record here – again). Having not started a league game all season, Lambert's appearance once again stressed not only the injury problems that the club had faced but also the chasm in resources between the clubs. Robson however had absolutely no doubts about the man, describing him as 'the perfect sub because he always came on and did things'. What he needed to do here was to keep running and keep the ball. We had 12 minutes.

It's fair to say that most of the country (outside of the red part of North London) were similarly willing us on through those 12 minutes. For us though they dragged to breaking point and, even though I can look at the game now and it appears that the players had it under control, that gripping fear borne of multiple disappointments convinced me otherwise right up until the whistle blew. IT BLEW. It was done. Watching Mick Mills ascend the stairs and pick up the cup almost seemed like it was unreal – a picture that had run through our minds so many times before but as a day dream rather than an observation.

The programme for the Final had set up the game very neatly for us – 'In recent seasons Ipswich Town have been plagued by an apparent inability to translate their undoubted class into a major honour. That can all end today in their first Wembley appearance.' The fact that this script had for once been followed was harder to grasp. The reality that we had won the cup took a while to sink in.

Not for the first time Mick Mills put it rather better than most. In a Radio Orwell interview just hours after the game he said that 'there have been many players that have gone through the Ipswich Town books over the last six or seven years that have deserved what those twelve players got today - plus a lot of people that have worked for the club. By us winning that trophy today they can look towards it as part of their own achievement and now I think that people will say that Ipswich Town have been great for seven years not just today'. This was a key point that was not lost on all supporters and probably many commentators too. The silverware was long overdue.

In the wider football world, it was considered a major shock and many were forced to eat their words. In the run up to the game, few had given Ipswich much of a chance, seemingly contracting amnesia about the last few seasons of this team and simultaneously dazzled by the apparent brilliance of our illustrious opponents.

As Arsenal headed into their 9th FA Cup Final and we broke our duck, commentators in the run up to the game seemed in little doubt about the outcome. Football Magazine's Cup Final special promised that 'Arsenal's sweet free flowing football is certain to add a touch of style to this season's FA Cup Final' whilst the (London) Evening News was typically non partisan (we might have felt honoured to be sharing the same pitch as the Gunners) – 'The spirit of Arsenal hangs over Wembley as it does over British soccer. For Arsenal and the awesome marble halls of Highbury is the essence of the game'. The News' competitor in London – The Standard – had no alternative view either as Michael Hart described Arsenal as having emerged as 'one of the most complete and entertaining teams in the country'.

The Arsenal players had been scarcely less self-assured. Pat Rice wrote in the Evening News that 'Ipswich promise us a hard game at Wembley. I have one answer to that. They are in for a harder one. The mood of the team is completely right. If we play like I know we can, we will win'. In particular, Rice saw the strength of the Arsenal midfield as the potential key. The Standard's Michael Hart agreed and he predicted that Liam Brady may use his lazy dummy 'with devastating effect against a sometimes stereotyped and inhibited Ipswich midfield' – what sophisticated and meaningless language. Rice's confidence seemed to transcend key personnel because he felt that 'no matter who fills the midfield spots for us, they will produce the most skilful and best balanced outfit in the league'; Terry Venables (then Palace's manager) similarly saw the 'skill and artistry' of the Arsenal midfield as their 'main strength'. Rice was rather dismissive in comparing this glittering Arsenal line up with Ipswich's which 'seems to be based more on power than skill'.

Trevor Brooking profiled the players in a head-to-head. His view of the midfield battle facing Roger Osborne was probably as appropriate a comment on the expectations of the football establishment as any – 'It is likely to be Roger's job to 'look after' Brady in midfield. I don't envy him his job. He sneaks in with the occasional goal but I sense that he will be working overtime on midfield duties'. No italics (or irony) required. History underlines which midfielder's name is associated with 1978.

There had been other player tussles highlighted. Bobby Robson was an admirer of Malcolm Mcdonald not just because of the big striker's obvious prowess and heritage over recent years but also because Robson had seen something so early when he and Harry Haslam bought him (as a defender) from Southern League Tonbridge (now Tonbridge Angels) to Fulham. Mcdonald's previous cup final appearance had delivered little and he was focused on making up for lost time; he promised that 'this time I'm determined to leave Wembley with a winner's medal' and his captain predicted that 'Malcolm and Frank Stapleton will give Hunter and Beattie a torrid time.' Beattie however later described the afternoon as 'the easiest game I'd played in for a long time' which underlined Allan Hunter's pre-match prediction that 'we know that Mcdonald will try extra hard to get a goal or two against us but there's no way we are going to let him through'. The evidence is there – Mcdonald barely had a shot on goal.

There had however been some recognition of the strengths of Robson's side in the lead up to the match. Rice acknowledged that 'no defence felt safe' from the Mariner and Whymark partnership and also pointed out that Woods 'can be a match winner' (he was right as Woods would justifiably be named Man of The Match.) This was however low key stuff by comparison and when it came to predicting a winner, few demurred from the general line (although many agreed only on the basis of their head over their heart.) The Express' David Miller and Trevor Brooking were notable exceptions.

An FA Cup Final appearance was however rightly acknowledged as just reward for Robson himself and it is therefore particularly apt that the famous victory has been greatly attributed to his tactical nous. Before the game, Paul Buckman in the Evening Standard had described him as a Master Tactician. This was especially prophetic for Wembley. The key to victory was Robson's decision to assign Osborne to pick up Brady and for Geddis (who was playing his only full 90 minutes of the season as he was third choice behind the injured Whymark and Turner) to play on the right so as to snuff out Nelson's service to the midfield. The insight for the decision came from Cyril Lea and Bobby Ferguson's research and the three worked together on the plan that turned out to be critical to the outcome. It is amazing to think that the side had never played this five man midfield formation before and had only known about it for the few days leading up to the final.

Some (sour grape sourced) comments suggested that the Manager had played a little gamesmanship with the late naming of Beattie and Hunter that day although Beattie himself has no truck for such accusations. In describing them as 'rubbish', Beattie points out that within a week both players were in hospital. In any event he had only made it through the final and the semi through the cortisone injections which, in due course, largely contributed to the end of his career.

Regardless of their near evangelical attachment to Arsenal or any mischievous accusations of gamesmanship, even the London press recognised the huge achievement of Robson in reaching the final. The Evening News accurately described Robson as 'intense and thoughtful', 'disciplined and with a lot of character.' For Robson himself though, there was no basking in the glory of making the final. He stressed that there would be no glory in coming second. Whilst much of the football establishment felt the outcome of the game to be almost a forgone conclusion and that Ipswich's role would be that of gallant losers, the Manager was far more ambitious. Any suggestion that they would enjoy the day regardless was rebuffed – 'we're going to go there very determined to win the cup. If we win the cup we will then enjoy the day'.

Robson's pre match talk was similarly focused and based on the simple message that 'we only have one chance and we don't want to come back in here with any regrets about what we didn't do'.

This focus and determination was shared by the players. In the club's Wembley '78 brochure, Allan Hunter felt that 'man for man I think that we're at least the equal of Arsenal. You could say I'm quietly confident' whilst Brian Talbot echoed his manager in emphasising that 'we'll go there knowing that we can win and no one should be surprised if we do'. In an interview with the Evening News (and to a rather less familiar readership), Mick Mills similarly sounded a battle cry by pointing out that 'to listen to what some people say, you would think that Arsenal only have to turn up at Wembley and the cup is theirs. I think that they are going to be in for the shock of their lives'. He rather astutely highlighted that all of this media praise might turn out to be a negative for the Gunners – 'there is nothing like complacency to destroy a team's chances of winning' – and Alan Sunderland later confirmed that that had indeed been a factor on the day and that Town had deservedly won.

If the club and team were considered low profile by comparison to their London counterparts, probably the lowest profile of all was Roger Osborne. Before the game he described getting to Wembley as being 'the biggest thing that's ever likely to happen to me'. Ninety minutes later and he had cause to think again.

Osborne's modesty was probably understandable as his route to Wembley was a decidedly low key affair. Having originally been at Ipswich merely to give his brother a lift to trials (a task to add to his day job as a builder), he was asked to play for the reserves in the midst of an injury crisis when he was 21 (the same age that Wembley Man Of The Match Clive Woods first had a trial). Ipswich born and bred, he'd grown up 'being' Crawford and Phillips in the playground; he was one of us. Actually he was much more. In a career that spanned 127 appearances over 7 years, he earned his presence alongside much bigger names. Robson was certainly an admirer of his virtues ('single minded, uncomplicated and dependable' with a 'great appetite for hard work') and had found the selection dilemma for the final a difficult one in comparing these with Colin Viljoen's vision and skills. In devising the tactics for the day, he knew that Osborne was the man for the job and, whatever the rights and wrongs of the Villa debacle, he also knew what the others felt about Osborne.

A 'fairy tale ending' was for once an entirely appropriate description of the outcome and a job well done. In Paul Mariner's words twenty years after the event – 'he nullified Brady and popped up with the goal. It couldn't have happened to a nicer guy.' For us supporters, maybe the script was that much more romantic because the match winner was an engine room man. The press had largely taken the obvious position on the outcome so for us it was the underdog's underdog who had the last laugh and that was precious.

The players' meagre (at least by today's standards) reward of a £4000 win bonus was supplemented by one or two little wagers which these days would be the subject of all sorts of investigations and disciplinary action but then were simply seen as a way of putting your money where your confidence is. If the bookies (along with the media) thought that Town were no hopers then why not take their cash when we prove them wrong? At odds of five to two, the £50 for each player that Mills and Robson put on Town to win turned out to be a nice surprise for them. Kevin Beattie went a step further by selling some of the player's complimentary tickets to a tout – the mind boggles.

Those players deserved all of the rewards going. It is easy to forget the season that they'd had or that several were playing through severe injuries and pain (especially Kevin Beattie). Similarly, the pitch hadn't helped. The match was actually in danger of being postponed because of the constant rain in the days leading up to the final and on the morning of the day itself. The sun however made an appearance – as if on cue – in the afternoon and this rather odd combination of a heavy pitch and sizzling heat resulted in the players losing six or seven pounds over the ninety minutes.

In view of the achievement and the fact that it was against the odds, it's good to note that there were plenty of plaudits flying about to supplement the financial rewards. They must have had some real currency with a team – and, let's be honest, a club – that stuffed a few prejudices down people's throats. Alan Hoby's Express' match report put it succinctly – 'Arsenal were clinically and almost contemptuously played off the Wembley pitch'. The same writer evoked memories of Sir Stanley Matthews in describing Woods' brilliant performance. He also considered it 'incredible' that Arsenal's 'luck stretched into the second half' before conceding a goal. Certainly the woodwork saved them from a much heavier defeat and to this day, like most of us, George Burley marvels at Pat Jennings' extraordinary save from his header, saying that 'it never ceases to amaze me that he managed to get his right hand to the ball'. In short, it could have been much worse for Arsenal.

Robson too won admirers in high places. The decision to appoint him jointly responsible for the England Under 21's – alongside his old pal Don Howe – was a notable bi-product of the Wembley victory, the significance of which would become crystal clear some four years later. That he was to continue to work with Don Howe – Arsenal's Coach in 1978 – would have been a particular pleasure. Twenty five years later Robson, aged 70, paid tribute to Howe as a lifetime friend going way back to his playing days at WBA. In particular, Robson was appreciative of Howe's unstinting support during his merciless hounding by the gutter press in his England days (which he described in 2003 as 'ridiculous, outrageous and obscene.')

I doubt that any praise would have meant more to Robson than that of his Dad who described the Cup Final win as 'the greatest moment of my life and I was so proud of Bobby. It was also a great family occasion because his four brothers were there to share it with him.' Little were his parents to know that this was just the start of a career that would make him the most widely successful and admired English manager ever. Their pride must have been immeasurable.

Widespread recognition of the manager, the team and the club was sweet indeed. Beyond the delirious joy for all Town supporters was the fact that – in Alan Hoby's words – this was a 'classic upset by a small town team whose victory can do nothing but good for the game.' This was very true but for many of us we were jealously holding onto the glory for ourselves.

There was too significant recognition for the fans' performance on the day. Much like the players, it had been expected that Town fans would be second best – in effect, silent partners in the atmosphere department but nothing could have been further from the truth. At the celebratory dinner after the match, players lined up to pay tribute. Allan Hunter admitted that the barrage of blue and white noise 'bought tears to my eyes' and was 'something that I'll cherish for the rest of my life'. Brian Talbot (a veteran of the terraces himself as a Town supporter) attributed some of the success to the fans when he said 'as well as we played on the field, they were as good off the field in cheering'; George Burley thought very simply that they had been the 'best I've ever heard'. Years later, Paul Mariner described the feeling of emerging from the tunnel and seeing the blue and white as convincing the players – 'we knew we wouldn't get beat as it just carried us all the way through'. Robson too considered that the fans' 'vocal support on the day was a vital factor in our triumph' and that 'the open top parade through the town culminating in those incredible scenes on the Cornhill [were] as much a highlight as the previous day at Wembley'.

All over Suffolk I am sure that school kids on Monday 8th May 1978 bustled in to school with their minds racing and their mouths yelling. I doubt however that there were many whose swagger was more pronounced than a 16 year old heading into a Kent School to be met by a few well wishers and a torrent of resentment. It was a great moment – a personal moment for me. There was no denying the arrival of our club now; despite all the evidence of the last five or so years, now we had the silverware, we'd done it in the national spotlight and we'd taken it from underneath the noses of one of our 'betters'. It didn't need to be screamed although I probably took the opportunity anyway!

Arsenal and Ipswich have a significant historical connection because it was Samuel Hill-Wood who took Ivan Cobbold to see Arsenal – a visit that inspired Ivan to form Ipswich Town FC. Maybe this should position Town as a nursery club (in the modern vernacular) or maybe what happened in 1978 was just messing too much with the natural order. Either way, to this day, some Arsenal supporters appear to be stung by it.

A few years ago when Town were in the Premiership and played Arsenal at Portman Road, my mate and I were having a pizza before the game when a couple of Arsenal supporters at the next table leant across and said that they still couldn't believe how we'd won in 1978. I'd have pointed it out to them – we were

MUCH better than you on the day – but I thought that if they'd not figured it out after 25 years it's probably a bit late now. It seems odd that they can't see it in perspective. We do. It was our day and they have had many many more. The chasm between the two clubs is now – and has been for years – enormous and undeniable. Arsenal are an admirable club and their football these days (and for some time actually) can be poetic. On that day however the last word was unequivocally and historically ours.

Onward To Europe

We headed in to the summer of 1978 by watching the FA Cup being presented by the players on a lap of honour at Portman Road – complete with a Suffolk Punch making the same trip. The occasion was Mick Lambert's testimonial game just three days after the final. I remember nothing whatsoever about the game – it was a night to relax and view the spoils of victory now that the gut wrenching tension of the day was a thing of the past. The crowd numbers that night were undoubtedly swollen by the opportunity to view the famous trophy and it proved a well deserved windfall for one of the club's loyal, no-nonsense and low key servants over 10 years at Portman Road. In particular, it might have been seen as poetic recognition for a key performance on the road to the cup when Lambert replaced the injured Brian Talbot at Highbury in the semi-final and worked tirelessly to close down Derek Statham of West Brom who had been widely recognised as a major threat. It was a typical, almost cameo-like, performance of enormous importance.

The glory of Wembley wasn't about to fade throughout the summer but at Portman Road there was work to be done in preparing for the 1978/79 season. There were several hugely significant consequences of the injury crisis that decimated the team throughout the previous season and these would play a major part in reshaping the next few years.

Firstly there was the emergence of Russell Osman, a former captain of the England schools rugby team. The 18-year-old had racked up 28 first team appearances in the previous season as deputy for Kevin Beattie and had turned some heads. Yet another product of the Youth set up – he had arrived as an apprentice in August 1975 and had been part of the Youth Cup winning side – he was still young and learning. Indeed, in 1976/77 he acknowledged that he needed to work on his heading, pace and timing in the tackle. The results of this were seen very quickly as he slotted in alongside Allan Hunter the very next season.

Indeed, such was his progress that there may have been a decision to be made for Robson come the Final. It was however a sign of Osman's maturity and attitude that he accepted Beattie being picked ahead of him, saying after the final that 'No one was more aware of Kevin's terrific value to the team than yours truly. He was fit so he had to play. I couldn't argue with that. If I'd been the manager I'd have done the very same. Mind you I'm not saying that I wasn't disappointed at missing out but I felt no bitterness whatsoever'. I imagine that Robson would have seen in this exactly the right sort of no-nonsense attitude that he was looking for – and that we as supporters would admire so much in the coming years.

The Manager may have had cause to value Osman – rather more than the other young jewels of the Youths - as Osman had been discovered not by the fabulously consistent Town scouting network but by Robson's own brother, Tom who had spotted the young Osman playing in a school match and identified him as 'another Kevin Beattie'.

As is so often the case with success stories, there was a parallel downside in that Dale Roberts would have been the first choice deputy for Beattie but was injured hence Osman was the one who made his first team claim – Roberts though would go on to have a long and much respected association with the club and be very much instrumental in its return to the top echelons of the game in 2000.

Secondly, changes in the midfield caused by John Wark's injuries created an opportunity for Eric Gates to shine. His 20 appearances in 1977/78 announced his arrival and gave us all a sign of what was to come. His eventual emergence was largely a question of tactics – in effect, positioning him in a slot that made sense in the overall shape of the team. When he did arrive as a first team regular it was in a very different system that the ever aware Robson had fashioned with an eye on mixing European vision and ball control with British athleticism. This perfectly suited the skills of Gates – his electric pace and explosive finishing sitting just behind the traditional front man.

Thirdly, Trevor Whymark's long reign as one of the first names on the team-sheet was coming to an end because of terrible luck with injuries. It is an absolute tragedy that his name has been almost downgraded when talking about the Robson years simply because of his absence from the Wembley team. Injury had decimated his season in 1977/78 to just nineteen league appearances and would be even worse in 1978/79 (just eight league appearances). As a measure of his significance, at the time of his injury (torn ligaments in a match at Carrow Road on Boxing Day 1977), he'd scored eighteen in the last twenty five.

Beyond that current form, such had been his contribution during the previous five years as Robson built his and the club's reputation that, but for the injuries, it would have been unthinkable that his name wouldn't be associated with the greatest moment in the club's history. Paul Cooper later said of Whymark's exclusion from Wembley that 'Trevor was a good player, a good servant and he was unlucky. The lads tried to cheer him up by telling him he might have another chance but it was no consolation'. That was understandable – his partnership with Mariner had been key to much of what was best about Town and practically the only people happy to see it disrupted would have been opposition defences.

For us supporters at the beginning of 1978/79 it was hard to envisage a forward line without Trevor Whymark – others came and went but the front two pairings with Johnson, Belfitt and Mariner had always been about their chemistry with Whymark. By early 1979 however he had departed for Vancouver Whitecaps but not before signing off with the winner in his own testimonial match against Norwich.

David Geddis had emerged as the most frequent deputy for Whymark the previous season and had of course capped his season with that cross at Wembley to underline a fine performance overall. Robson later described him as being 'full of determination and aggression' and highlighted his pace as being 'a great asset'. Indeed, Geddis had announced his arrival as early as the very first game of the last season by scoring the winner against Arsenal but, if we assumed that he was the heir apparent to Whymark, the 1978/79 season would prove us wrong. Geddis would make just 6 appearances (his career later blossomed elsewhere but really took off in coaching as he later became part of the set up both at Newcastle and under Sven-Goran Erickson for England) but a young Scotsman would emerge from nowhere to claim the position alongside Mariner for several seasons to come.

Alan Brazil, like Kevin Beattie before him, had been invited to a trial at Ipswich without any knowledge of the club or the town. His response to Town scout George Findlay's invitation was positive but accompanied by the question 'where is it?' Having made his way down from his native Glasgow he soon found out and would spend an explosive five years at the club, arriving as an 18 year old in 1977 amidst the hullabaloo of the FA Cup season. He set his stall out pretty much immediately by being voted the S. E. Counties League Player of The Year. The fact that he had joined what was an extraordinarily successful Youth team set up under Charlie Woods which had, just a season earlier, won both the South East Counties League and League Cup made this impact all the more noteworthy.

Competition was tough at Ipswich then – the only three youth players from the 1976/77 squad to be offered professional terms were Brazil, Russell Osman and Terry Butcher. This was a reflection both of the success of the process but also of the inevitable losers in a scheme that developed the cream of the crop and therefore had no place for those that weren't quite there. Whilst Osman made his mark immediately, Brazil had to wait till 1978/79 to rack up his first seventeen appearances - and his first nine goals.

Some new faces were arriving – and things were changing for some established ones too. There was apparent evidence that Wembley success had upped the profile of several Town players for whom offers were being made. Chief amongst these was Brian Talbot who was the subject of overtures from Arsenal. Robson was unequivocal on the subject. James Lawton in the Express recounted Robson saying that 'I'm telling Talbot quite simply that he is staying at Ipswich for three years – the length of his current contract – at least'. Although the move was averted in the short-term, changes in personnel elsewhere paved the way for its delayed completion in 1979 although not before Talbot had put in some great performances including one against Innsbruck in the Cup Winners Cup when Talbot – playing through injury – put 'two matches into one for us' according to Robson. Overall though Talbot acknowledged the effect of the speculation on his own game and maybe Robson concluded that a player who wants to be somewhere else – however important they've been to the side – was of reduced value. Whatever the reasons, Talbot went on to a glittering career with the Gunners including two further consecutive FA Cup Final appearances after 1978 – a very distinguished hat-trick.

Rumours of player unrest were undoubtedly unsettling and Robson was quick to point out the need for such players to appreciate what the club had done for them as much as what they'd done for the club. His words in 1979 seem startlingly prophetic – 'you look around the game and you can come to the conclusion that too many players are thinking more about money than football'.

Another player being much feted by the 'big' clubs was Paul Mariner – now established not only as one of the best strikers in the English league but also as an England centre forward of stature. Here though the news was much better. Mariner summed up his position very neatly at the time - 'I saw my name being linked with just about every top club in the country. But what they seemed to forget was that I was already at a top club. As far as I'm concerned they don't come any better. Since the day I arrived at Portman Road I've been happy and I believe that there are a lot more good times around the corner.' As supporters, there would be little better in the good news department for us.

The most welcome example of stability amongst all of the changes was the continued presence of the man himself. Robson's stock had been high for years and he had resisted several approaches from other clubs but the Cup win would have significantly increased the temptation for him and tested the resolution of the Board.

Sunderland, Barcelona and Atletico Bilbao were amongst the suitors. Not that Robson was in any doubt about the importance of loyalty – how could he be? It is the very essence of the man and underpinned the strength of his position at Portman Road. He said of the Cobbold brothers - 'if it wasn't for these two men I wouldn't be at Ipswich today'. This presumably recognised their courage in appointing him as an unknown Manager, their loyalty to him when things were going badly and his equivalent loyalty to them when opportunities later arose that could have taken him to more money, prominence and – let's be honest – chances of trophies. Robson's own innate appreciation of these virtues was backed up by a letter that he had received from the great Stan Cullis which very simply advised him 'not to leave a chairman who backs you in everything you do'. Fair point – such animals were rare then and are virtually extinct today.

It should be remembered that Robson's role at the football club went well beyond the playing field. For example, by 1978 the club had spent over £1.5m on ground improvements which were in Robson's words, 'sensibly funded' (by the end of 1978/79 the club's accounts would show a record £200,000 profit.) Again, echoes of a time when solid principles ruled over rampant ego's and megalomania.

The seeds of change were sown that season via a mix of the Portman Road Youth 'conveyor belt' and some visionary dealing in the transfer market.

The significance of the former cannot be overestimated and Robson was rightfully proud of it. In 1978 he told the (London) Evening Standard 'I've got five good friends – some may call them scouts. One each in Scotland, Wales, the North East, Sheffield and London. They're called Marconi; if anyone gets to know their real names I'm done for'. The radar systems worked spectacularly well. In addition to Ray Tyrrel working locally to find players like Brian Talbot, we know that at least a couple of the Marconi's were in fact John Carruthers and George Findlay. The crucial point though is that the system was operated by Chief Scout Ron Gray (once the youngest manager in the Football League at Watford in 1948) hand in hand with Robson who, in this regard, had every right to call Ipswich 'his' club.

Alongside Robson's belief and participation in the Youth policy was his attitude to spending in the transfer market. He explained - 'you've got to realise that I spend the club's money as if it were my own'. The suggested frugality supported justifiable pride in his track record. Quite apart from unearthing stars from the youth system such as Burley, Beattie and Wark, he had bought hugely important players such as Cooper and Hunter for relative peanuts. He later described this same attitude to money when he was working at clubs like Barcelona where funds were in a different world – but the basics of doing things right remained the same.

The most startling aspect of 1978/79 – amongst the departures, graduation of youths and arrival of some new faces – was that Robson and his staff would literally transition one great side into another. At the beginning of 1978/79, whilst this transition wasn't clear to us, some of the elements were in front of our eyes and, had we but known it, they signalled the dawning of a very new chapter in Robson's Ipswich years.

****

On the field, the season could hardly have got off to a more inauspicious start. A 0-5 mauling by Forest in the Charity Shield at Wembley was every bit as one sided as the Cup Final had been and even the absence of Osborne, Beattie, Hunter and Geddis could hardly be seen as mitigation.

Early in the new season saw the latest, and maybe most significant, development - the arrival of a little known Dutchman called Arnold Muhren. Negotiations were underway as the season kicked off but were not concluded in time for him to play the full season and he therefore missed the first two games. A former Ajax player (and team-mate of Cruyff, Neeskins and Rep), he joined from FC Twente and he knew about Ipswich both from having played against them and from watching them – not least in the Wembley glory day.

Robson's vision in bringing in a cultured midfielder was tactically reminiscent of his most famous predecessor at Portman Road. Sir Alf Ramsay created a team around the deep use of overlapping midfielders which confused teams expecting the conventional winger formation. Robson, always a studious tactician, obviously saw the potential to fundamentally change the way that the midfield operated and thereby to remould the team. The later departure of Talbot was no doubt a significant element of this as his extraordinary 'engine room' was replaced by Muhren's vision and distribution. Muhren himself saw the significance. He described the Dutch game as 'like chess with more players involved in every move' (this no doubt suited Muhren who Terry Butcher described on meeting him as 'quiet, shy and studious') and he realised that this was out of step with the British game where there 'seems to be a tendency to hit the strikers a lot earlier' by playing 'direct from defence without using the midfield players'. The potential clash of these two styles would do no one any favours – they had to be skilfully melded together to reap the benefit of both and that was Robson's genius.

Whilst Muhren was not the first overseas player to arrive on the English stage (Ardiles and Villa had very recently arrived at

White Hart Lane), his effect on the Ipswich Town side over the next three years was as significant as any. It would take time for this to become clear to the world but Robson knew it from the off. It was his vision and his piercing intelligence that made it happen. The transfer was no easy deal either – Robson later describing it as 'one of the most difficult transactions of my career here'. Muhren needed persuading and, despite the club laying 'out the red carpet', the initial answer was a no. It was only later when Muhren reflected on the offer that he changed his mind – Robson believed that what made the difference were 'the lengths we had gone to and the area that he was coming to. He also wanted a challenge and felt certain he would settle quickly'.

On the field though, two straight defeats in the first league games – conceding five along the way – didn't improve things after the Charity Shield fiasco. In particular a 0-3 reverse to Liverpool at Portman Road in a night game was a sobering affair. Like many I had been looking forward to the unveiling of Arnold Muhren but that event was overshadowed by a brilliant Liverpool performance. Muhren later said that the only time that he saw the ball was when he looked up to see it sail over his head and that's about right. Town had not yet figured out how to use the Dutchman and, to make matters worse, they were up against a Liverpool side at the top of their game. The journey back home was a long one as I spent it in a standing-room-only train carriage full of excited Scousers en route back to London. My silence probably did much to alert them to my affinity but when we finally got into conversation they were – as I have generally found them to be – open, warm and appreciative of good football. On that night all of the examples of the latter came from Liverpool but it wouldn't always be that way.

If we were looking for some evidence that the new Robson

vision would work it came just five days later with a 3-0 win over Manchester United. The manager made a public statement of intent – 'I bought him [Muhren] to be a playmaker. It is going to take about five games to get Muhren bedded in. At the end of this process you will see clearly where we are going.' The Express' James Lawton saw signs there and then – 'when he [Muhren] makes contact with the ball the Robson initiative makes such dramatic sense'. Alongside a great performance and two goals from Mariner as well as a 'performance of splendour' from Beattie, this result did much to point the way forward.

And yet that result was the exception rather than the rule. By the beginning of November we were still only fifteenth. Results weren't coming in the short-term. Two-legged victories over AZ67 and Innsbruck ensured Cup Winners Cup progress but things weren't working out on the home front.

The pressure was telling and Robson – rather uncharacteristically – spoke to the press about potentially calling it a day. His reasons were simple. He told James Lawton of the Express - 'I believe that a football manager's value can only be measured by the effect he is having on a group of players at any one time. At this moment, I'm not having any effect'. These are stark words the truth of which is indisputable. Many a good manager has walked – or been shown the door – because their impact was on the wane for reasons that may be no fault of their own. In this case Robson thought that it may be over familiarity. His view that 'I know I won't get the sack at this place' suggested that the friendly environment that had done so much to create the success of the last seven or eight years was now potentially stifling – the heart and grit was missing.

It's impossible to say whether the manager's words had that elusive affect on the players but the results and performances did start to pick up. Four wins from the next seven (including, in Robson's words, a 'vintage Ipswich' performance at Maine Road) lifted the gloom and 1979 as a whole told pretty much a completely different story including twelve wins from twenty games with five back to back throughout April.

A very significant element was the fact that Osman played almost a full season deputising for the injured Hunter who never really recovered from the injury that threatened his cup final. For the first half of the season, Osman partnered Beattie until Beattie's season was once again decimated by injury. This created an opening for one Terry Butcher and, though all three would play together a few times that season, the real effect was the passing of the old guard. The 'bacon and eggs' partnership of Hunter and Beattie was being replaced by a partnership that would take centre stage in the next chapters of the Robson years.

Most of us knew little about Butcher. It would have been instructive at the time to have known that he'd had a trial at Norwich and that the experience of wearing that kit had almost made him 'physically sick' Born in Singapore where his dad was stationed in the navy, the family moved back to Lowestoft (from where his parents had originated) in 1960 when Butcher was just two and so the Suffolk and England stalwart was established.

The Norwich trial was unwelcome because, by that time, there was only one side that Butcher wanted to play for since his passion for Portman Road had been fed by visits with his dad. In 1975, at the age of 17, he got his chance when signing a £50 a week professional deal. Graduating through those successful Youth sides (including winning the S.E Counties league in 1976/77 in a side that contained 40 goal Alan Brazil), he arrived at the reserves under the stewardship of Bobby Ferguson who he described as a 'hard taskmaster who wanted the best out of you and wasn't prepared to hang about to see if time would make you a better player'.

It's odd to relate now but Butcher's initial problem was a lack of aggression. With some uncompromising coaching, the fearless centre half who we would all soon admire emerged and in April 1978 he made his first team debut. His three appearances in 1977/78 were a precursor to his fully fledged arrival in 1978/79.

Just how quickly Osman and Butcher settled can be measured by Robson's comments after a March 1979 draw with Forest in which Trevor Francis – then the country's first £1m player - made his debut. The manager said – 'There was a time when I was worried about us when we were without Beattie but not anymore. Both Osman and Butcher are accomplished young players and neither of them were the slightest bit concerned about Francis making his debut.'

The emergence of Muhren – alongside the rather less planned injuries to the central defensive partnership - was the catalyst behind Robson's overall reshaping of the side. There was however another angle about to be unveiled when, at the end of February 1979, we welcomed our second Dutch midfielder to Portman Road. Frans Thijssen arrived from FC Twente for £220,000 – Robson's most expensive purchase. A former team mate of Muhren's, Thijssen's skills were entirely complimentary and had been noticed by Robson when Town had played Twente in the UEFA cup; the manager had seen the potential of combining Thijssen's almost magnetic ball control and possession with Muhren's vision and passing capabilities. It was as good an example of Robson's astute judgement as we ever saw. What's more, the 27-year-old Thijssen did his chances of instant hero worship no harm at all by recording his first goal as the winner at Carrow Road.

Robson's vision and tenacity in securing the Dutch duo was matched by his business nous. He said of the deals – 'The transfer market in this country had gone quite absurd and I'm convinced that we got two class players for less than I would have had to pay for one ordinary one'. There can be no argument on that score.

As much as these changes looked good (and, in retrospect, were critical), at the time the day-to-day was still giving us little to smile about. By late March hopes of retaining the FA Cup had been extinguished by Liverpool and interest in the Cup Winners Cup had been cruelly ended on away goals by Barcelona following an aggregate 2-2 in which Eric Gates had scored the decisive goal in a 2-1 win at Portman Road.

What made the season was an unbeaten run for the last 11 games. Brazil's role in this was significant – he had largely been used as a substitute until Christmas but from February appearances and goals started to flow and he finished the season with the number nine shirt for the last straight six games scoring seven goals along the way. Everyone took notice – even those of us who'd grown out of the need to 'be' a player in the playground and who were therefore no longer looking for the new Jimmy Robertson or David Johnson.

A sixth place finish and qualification for Europe erased the early season jitters and Robson's suggestion that his time at Portman Road may have been up. The season was rounded off with a 4-0 away win at QPR; the score sheet reflected the significant change of faces that had taken place during the season – Gates 2, Butcher and Brazil.

Muhren was voted Player of The Year which was not only a symbol of the Dutchman's immediate impact but also of Robson's vision. Importantly though, alongside the new faces were several rocks of the previous years – Woods, Wark, Burley, Cooper and Mills played 100% or near as damn it that season so Robson was in the process of successfully blending the established with the new. Despite some traumas along the way – none greater than the threat of Robson's departure – the season had been more than turned around. Out of adversity had come a new shape of team for a new era although we weren't yet aware of it.

****

Town fans were used to roller coaster rides. Throughout our years at the top we never seemed to have seasons of consistent point hauls. Though we shared those top table positions with the likes of Liverpool, their prominence seemed to be built on a relentless collection of points whether playing well or not. How often have we heard expounded the theory that what makes a champion side is the ability to win when playing badly? There was never such consistency at Ipswich which is why 1979/80 – a season in which we were to enjoy our equal highest finish since returning to the top flight over ten years earlier – yielded just four wins out of the first fifteen league games. Bottom of the league in October.

The loss of Clive Woods to injury changed the shape of the team as, without a conventional winger, Mariner and Brazil (now the natural front pairing) were looking for supply from different areas. Bringing Gates into a position just behind them and encouraging the midfielders forward would create a different supply route and maybe once again play to the strengths of the new Dutchmen. Be that as it may, the loss of Woods was a major blow – his speed and trickery had continued to mesmerise defences throughout the previous season ensuring that his day at Wembley in 1978 was neither a swansong nor the prime moment for which he is appreciated by the fans. 1979/80 would turn out to be his final season of a ten year career at Ipswich during which he had become such a critical part of the creativity of the team. His record of 338 appearances was testament to his consistency over a period of great change (he arrived at Ipswich in 1969 – the same year that Robson did). What says most about the fans admiration for the winger though is the fact that he was born in – and left to join – Norwich and yet still he is revered amongst us.

In many ways – and despite the plaudits for his day at Wembley – Woods was one of the teams lesser profile faces which maybe reflects a general change in the way that players and clubs were treated by the media. Whilst Mariner and Brazil were lively personalities who were both attracted to, and comfortable in, the limelight, such an environment was alien to many others including Mick Lambert who departed Portman Road in 1979 also after 10 years distinguished and much appreciated service which contributed so critically to the 1978 Cup campaign and much else. Roger Osborne would also be gone in 1980 after seven years – another example of that low key group but one whose moment in the sun is immortal.

So here we were languishing near the bottom of the league with a new looking team taking shape. Changes in the backroom can't have helped either – Cyril Lea leaving to go to Stoke after 15 years as player, coach and even caretaker manager. The reshuffle moved Bobby Ferguson from reserve to first team coach and Charlie Woods from youth to reserves. With changes in playing and coaching personnel maybe we had no right to expect the team to start out of the blocks the way that they'd finished the previous season but it was impossible to wonder whether the storming end to last season had been more a false dawn than a declaration of intent. Would this team gel and if so how long it would take?

Today, a manager has no time or second chances. The Cobbold's loyalty to Robson was undeniably critical to his long term success and their view was, at least in part, based on some simple common sense and humility – no one can win all the time. The longer that Robson was into his tenure, the more that we supporters appreciated the massive strides that he'd made – but equally and simultaneously we felt the frustration of missing out on the big prizes. It's no fun being forever the bridesmaid.

Sometimes it takes an outsider to put it best and a tribute to Robson from Bob Paisley in 1979 seems most apt – 'Bobby Robson is one of the most respected Managers in football. We have had many outstanding games with Ipswich and looking back over recent years one can only speculate that if the ball had run a little more kindly for them they would have won more honours than they have'. It's true that our haul so far was scant reward for the quality of the sides that Robson had produced. We still believed however and there was never any serious sign of the sort of clamour for change – from media and fans alike - that these days is inevitable after a string of poor results regardless of the wider context.

The early season run in 1979/80 was dismal and included a 1-4 mauling at Selhurst Park in late September by Terry Venables' 'team of the 80s' (that never quite was). That day was symptomatic of the first part of the season – we were outplayed and well off the pace throughout. The 'ole' moments that we'd enjoyed over the last few years and as recently as the run in to the end of the last season seemed a thing of the past as Palace seemed a yard faster in pace and several seconds ahead in thought. Most of us there that day were prompted to wonder, if Palace were the team of the 80s, were we going to be a relic of the past? It was a depressing day.

Most of us felt that the basis of the team was right and yet the results wouldn't come. Robson's faith was unshakeable and we can only surmise that hard work on the training field alongside personal reassurances came to fruition because the facts are that from the beginning of December to the end of the season Town lost only one game, drew seven and won sixteen! Quite extraordinary. Once again those dismal days were soon forgotten.

Behind the facts too were some breathtaking performances and statistics. Four goal hauls happened four times, the top four scorers (Mariner, Wark, Gates and Brazil) finished the season with a combined fifty four League goals, a 7-0 win was recorded in European competition (v Skeid Oslo in the UEFA Cup) and we only once conceded more than two goals.

Chief amongst the headlines in this period must go to an extraordinary result at Portman Road on March 1 1980 – Ipswich Town 6 Manchester United 0. Behind the headline lay an even more astonishing fact in that Town also managed to miss two penalties – although technically it was three as one was twice taken. The result might have suggested that Man United's keeper Gary Bailey – son of ex-Town keeper Roy – had had a nightmare but nothing was further from the truth as he'd saved all three penalties and was only really at fault for one of the goals. Town had just simply been on fire with the front two netting five between them – a hatrick for Mariner and a brace for Brazil (who acknowledged the importance of Muhren's service to the strikers in this game and many others). United were no mugs either as they'd come into the game in second place and would finish the season there. Looking at this result from 2009, it is hard to compute but it was a measure of how far Town had come under Robson that we saw it simply as one top team beating another because we both had realistic title ambitions.

As much as the strikers would grab headlines that season, some very belated recognition was also accorded Paul Cooper. Rather strangely, the keeper had been talked of in some quarters as the team's weak link because he was the only non-international in the side (more a reflection on England's riches in the goalkeeping department at the time than any comment on his abilities) and maybe simply wasn't a name. This seems another example of lazy journalism of the sort that is commonplace these days (the most obvious example being MOTD pundits making comments about newly promoted sides to the Premiership about which they know nothing whatever).

For us as fans, Cooper's value was always crystal clear. Robson considered signing Cooper to have been one of his 'best managerial decisions' and reflected on a number of attributes including 'wonderful agility, speed off the line, distribution and reliability'. What made 1979/80 the season of his public recognition though was an unbelievable record of saving eight out of ten penalties including two in the game against Derby that was covered by the BBC. Cooper himself has never spoken at length about his secret but certainly he studied potential penalty takers' style and his concentration must have been unshakeable.

The fact was that with Cooper between the posts there was a sense of security that we felt in the stands and that must have been critical to the defenders in front of him. Other managers and players too would later add their tribute and point out other attributes – future Town manager John Lyall (then at West Ham) highlighted his 'anticipation and agility' whilst Southampton's Chris Nicholl pointed to his 'positioning and handling'.

Most importantly, Cooper's contribution to the club's success – regardless of his personal profile – was being recognised and of course history would show that he was very far from finished.

He would go on to make no less than 575 appearances and take his place in the Ipswich Top Five of all time.

By the end of the season, once again, we had reason to cheer. Finishing third had once again kept us in that elite group alongside Liverpool, Manchester United, Arsenal and Forest at the top. Some new faces were beginning to appear too – Kevin O'Callaghan had arrived in a very high profile deal from Millwall, a young and fast winger whose presence was maybe intended to take the mantle from Clive Woods although it never quite did. We would once again be in Europe and our new look side had an exciting mix of the old and the new producing a blend of football that we'd not seen before – indeed that no one in England had seen before.

Finally, once again clubs came calling with a big cheque in an attempt to lure away Mr Robson. This time it was Barcelona. He publicly stated that he wanted to stay and finish the job he'd started at Ipswich but, in any event, Ipswich's compensation demands (rumoured to be £150,000) were unacceptable to the Catalans. The boldness of the club's position belied its relative strength but was, once again, a shot in the arm for all us supporters.

A year later Robson was honest in admitting that 'I wanted to go' for 'continental football, new faces, new players, new language' and money that was 'a chance of a lifetime'. What balanced this though was Robson's appreciation of the Cobbold's and their unstinting support of him – 'I thought that getting the sack at Fulham was the worst thing that ever happened to me but it was the best thing that ever happened to me because I came here'

It is a measure of Robson, the Cobbolds and the club at the time

ONWARD TO EUROPE

that there were no hard feelings from Robson (as with Mills earlier) that the Board in effect blocked the move. He balanced it out and cracked on. How perfect then that his greatest moment was just around the corner and that his great adventure – and towering success – in Europe was merely postponed.

****

1980/81 turned out to be historic and glorious – a 66 game marathon that could have yielded even more than it did. The haul of one enormous trophy has often been placed in context of the 'failure' to land the other two in a season when the treble of League, FA Cup and UEFA Cup was a real possibility. This is unfair and unrealistic – maybe we deserved more but what we got was the crowning achievement of a wonderful manager and an exceptional team. For me the sting in the tail was less about the trophies that we didn't win and more about the fact that European success probably finally raised Robson's profile that one last notch that made our hopes of his remaining at Portman Road impossibly forlorn. But that was maybe an inevitable price to pay for a small Suffolk market town conquering Europe.

We may all have had an early indication that this was to be a season to remember by the fact that it started with a fourteen game unbeaten run in the league. Compared to the spluttering start of the previous season, Town were out of the traps and on fire from the off, recording some spectacular results along the way including a 1-0 win over Villa (a significant result as the season would develop) and a 4-0 hammering of Everton.

The new look team was rather less new now. The defensive giants of Beattie and Hunter were limited to just eight combined league appearances whilst Osman recorded a 100% turnout in the league and Butcher was only just behind having played forty of forty two. Muhren played all but one league game whilst Thijssen played thirty one.

These statistics however belie the real story of the season which was ultimately one of stretched resources. Success in three competitions creates a fixture pile up that stretches squads to the limit and the effect on Ipswich was to blood some squad players in major games whether they were ready or not. Fifteen years later, Robson himself said that 'maybe we would have liked a larger squad of top players as opposed to fourteen or fifteen with some good reserves. With a top squad of eighteen you can survive, but you're relying on virtually the same team all the time'. In that season Robson put it quite simply – 'we just couldn't rest our key players'. This meant hoping that 'we keep everyone fit and we don't get injuries'. Such hopes are likely to end in disappointment and they did – the effect being seen as the season wore on.

The first league defeat though didn't come until November 11th (a 0-1 defeat at Brighton) by which time not only were Town the league pacesetters but they had already negotiated their way through two rounds of the UEFA Cup. In many ways these European games were a real barometer of the new look Robson side because his blend of European sophistry and British muscle/stamina was to be tested to its limit in situations and environments far more varied than those found in the English first division (as was).

A good example of this was the first round tie with Greek side Aris Salonika. There would have been few better portents for the campaign than a 5-1 win at Portman Road in the first leg – especially as it included no less than four from John Wark which incorporated a hat-trick of penalties (maybe his prior knowledge of the Greeks – his mother in law was from a small town near

Salonika – gave him extra heart). As was to be the case again though (and had been in the past), two legged ties aren't always settled by unequivocal first leg results. The penalty haul at Portman Road was, in Robson's view, a sign of the Greeks' approach to the game and his post match comments reflected that as well as sounding a warning for the second leg – 'they'll turn a game of football into a war with their tackling and intimidation'; he was however confident in predicting that 'if we play a good, open, sporting but tough British game out there we'll get out of it alright'.

He was right in that the 1-3 defeat in front of 40,000 gave Town a comfortable aggregate victory despite at one point trailing 0-3 making the aggregate look rather more threatening at the time especially with their away goal at Portman Road. In the end it was an Eric Gates goal that did the trick by effectively cancelling out the Greeks' away goal advantage.

Robson's confidence in his team's ability to battle and to keep their discipline (despite, according to Butcher, Salonika fans throwing things at them at training before the game and their coach windows being smashed afterwards) was well placed – the Aris Salonika game was a battle through which the side emerged victorious without ever having played the sort of football that they would have liked but it certainly earned them the chance to do so later. The Greek fans and media's antipathy towards Town was, according to John Wark, sparked by an orchestrated rumour that the referee in the Portman Road game had been bribed into the penalties and sendings off. A relatively cursory look at the film of the game dismisses this as nonsense; few refs would have done anything else.

The second round again gave us a home tie in the first leg, this time against Czech side Bohemians of Prague. Robson was a fan of the Czech game, commenting later that their teams were 'good, tough, durable' and with 'good technique'. Again then it would be important to build up a cushion in the home leg and that's exactly what happened with a fine 3-0 win which featured two more from Wark and a critical cameo appearance by substitute Kevin Beattie whose thunderbolt thirty-yard free-kick turned out to be the winner in the tie as the 3-0 home win was followed by a 0-2 away defeat on a freezing night. The away result was testament to a brilliant defensive performance in withstanding 'almost non-stop attacking pressure' (according to the Telegraph) including going behind after just two minutes.

Once again the star was Beattie but any hopes of this being a long-term return to defensive duties were premature; the Beat's role was no longer centre-stage but few supporting actors can have been so important especially in the UEFA Cup campaign.

Away from Europe, league form was not dramatically affected by the first defeat at the Goldstone Ground as the side went on to lose only one of the next seventeen with goals being contributed from forwards and midfielders alike (Thijssen, Wark and Muhren contributing twenty six goals between them for the season). This run also yielded a pretty healthy goals against column – it was a rare for anyone to put more than one past Cooper and his backline so the 3-5 defeat at White Hart Lane in December was quite an event.

Christmas 1980 was celebrated not only with Town continuing to set the pace in the league but also with a sweet 2-0 defeat of Norwich on Boxing Day – Brazil and Wark providing the perfect presents for Town supporters.

By that stage we were also celebrating negotiating another round in Europe, this time with a rather more unequivocal victory over Eastern European opposition in the form of Widzew Lodz of Poland. The Poles were hardly household names but they'd made quite a splash by removing Manchester United in the previous round and Robson later recalled that their confidence ('they must have thought that they've beaten Man Utd so they'll demolish Ipswich') was illustrated by their Manager wanting to place a little wager on the result. Robson though took all this in his stride. Once again he was aware of just how difficult the away leg would be hence the importance of building up a commanding lead in the home tie. His purring satisfaction of the 5-0 home win – 'we smashed them to smithereens' – was totally understandable. On the night there were some brilliant goals (including a Mariner diving header from a fantastic Muhren cross with the outside of his boot) and eye-catching performances including one from Steve McCall, one of the reserves whose opportunities rose that season because of the fixture congestion and whose performances earned him great admiration.

The away leg on December 10th probably shouldn't have been played – it was minus fourteen and the pitch was pretty much unplayable under ice – but Robson pragmatically accepted that, with a 5-0 advantage, it was better to play than to risk a postponement of three months so he accepted the opportunity to make a call. The slim 0-1 defeat – again the product of a resolute defensive performance - made no difference to the outcome.

The new year started with the opening salvo's in the third leg of the possible treble – an FA Cup third round home tie with Aston Villa. As two of the pacesetters in the league it was probably one of those 'tie of the round' candidates (cited by people who seem to miss the point that any game which is replicated in the league cannot possibly be so – it's the David v Goliath battles that have to earn that epithet). Paul Mariner's goal was enough to see Town through and it was to be one of three wins from three matches against Town's biggest rivals for the League Championship. This is a sobering statistic given that the trophy would ultimately go to Villa Park.

Consistency over this and previous seasons – culminating in some major silverware – meant that everyone now knew the name Ipswich Town. Maybe even I seemed a bit less of an oddity to my mates whose footballing affinities remained overwhelmingly London based.

As an 18-year-old I had graduated from family car journeys to the train and then to my own car as the means of delivering me to Suffolk. Over the years I would own a succession of often rather forlorn vehicles – one of them having an almost perennially knackered radiator which meant stopping two or three times during the journey to refill with water and then keeping an eye on the temperature gauge in readiness for the next one – but none would get in the way. In fact what was more likely to challenge for my time was an ever increasing interest in music; joining several bands and lugging my drum kit around in those same battered cars put a strain on time and money. But love is love and ITFC remained a constant.

The truth is that, with life developing around me, I am certain that I didn't appreciate the full significance of what was happening at Portman Road that season – which is saying something because I (like most Town fans) was on cloud nine for most of it.

Back in the league it was March 21st before Town lost a game in 1981 – scoring twenty six and conceding just six in ten games. That defeat came at Old Trafford and the statistics record that it was the start of the unravelling of the league season because Town would go on to win just two of their last nine games – a run that, in effect, undid much of the advantage built up by such extraordinary consistency displayed up until then.

During that period, Burley and Mills were often absentees as was Thijssen whilst Mariner and Gates too missed out on some of the critical games in the league run in. O'Callaghan, Tommy Parkin, Kevin Steggles, Mich D'Avray and Robin Turner all made brief appearances throughout the season whilst Steve McCall clocked up thirty four appearances in the league and nine in the UEFA Cup to move centre stage where he would remain for the next six years or so.

March was also a key month in the UEFA Cup where things were getting serious as we moved into the quarter final stage with a tie against the French giants St Etienne. Robson said fifteen years later that he had been 'semi-frightened' by what he saw when preparing for the game — a rare comment for a man always so positive in measuring his own teams against opposition.

It was easy to see his point because the French Champions, who included Rep, Platini and Battiston, were many people's tips for the final. Eric Gates though summed it up by telling Robson at the time — 'if we beat them now then we won't have to in the final' which is fair. The players themselves were clearly relishing the challenge and were high on the momentum of the campaign.

For the first time, Town would play away in the first leg and the 42,000 sell out crowd was in the ground early enough for gates to be locked two hours before kick off. In the tunnel, Butcher recalls giving 'it plenty' and seeing the French stars' nervousness at this 'team of lunatics'. Any of the French fans who were unconvinced by the pedigree of the opposition (who may have felt like Widzew Lodz's manager before the previous round) and were buoyed by their club's extraordinary record of never having lost at home in European competition over the last twenty six years, were in for as big a shock as their players.

Town turned on the style to record a 4-1 win. Robson hailed the result as 'arguably the best – certainly one of the best - English performances away in Europe of all time'. St Etienne's coach Robert Herbin was similarly fulsome in his praise – 'we were outclassed by a better team' – as were the English press of which The Telegraph's description of a 'classic exhibition of attacking soccer' was a good example. Indeed, the Telegraph picked out Muhren as having had a 'tremendous game' and, very perceptively, highlighted 'just how mature a team [Ipswich] have become over the last year' playing 'relaxed' and 'controlled' football. Given the pressure of the night that is some measure of the belief and discipline of this new Robson wonder team.

Muhren's sweet strike on the night was complemented by yet another from Wark and two from Mariner in what was a brilliant team performance – a team that included Steggles and McCall deputising in an XI that was beginning to show the strain of a long hard season. Heroes all. Back at Portman Road for the return Butcher, Wark and Mariner scored in a 3-1 win (Ipswich playing 'relaxed football which, at this stage of the competition, is something of a luxury' according to The Telegraph) to conclude an extraordinary 7-2 aggregate victory.

If an illustration were needed of the effects of the fixture congestion that season there can be few better than the two week period between 4th and 18th March. In between the first and second leg St Etienne ties came the little matter of an FA Cup quarter final at The City Ground Nottingham. On March 7th, I was one of a huge following packed into the away end to witness a quite extraordinary 3-3 draw in which we were 2-0 up but finally had to come back from 2-3 down to grab a replay. Despite the fact that this was as British a game as can be imagined – mostly blood and thunder – it was no coincidence that Thijssen supplied the equaliser and that both Dutchmen were prominent throughout. The mix was working.

Just three days later the replay at Portman Road was another corker but of a different kind – a tightly balanced match between two sides full of running and inventiveness was decided by a brilliant Muhren volley to send us into our first semi final of the season. There was an extraordinary feeling in the ground that night – the excitement was at fever pitch and however thick and fast the games came, the team just seemed to rise to the occasion. If we were all tempted now to look ahead to the St Etienne second leg, first there was an important home league game against Spurs (a decent side) to fit in four days after the FA Cup game and four prior to St Etienne. Result? – 3-0 with goals from Gates, Wark and Brazil.

The togetherness of the side was key. Behind the scenes, players seemed to thrive on the momentum of success. They also didn't appear to equate it with pressure. Years later Eric Gates said 'we didn't realise what a good squad we had. We were just a family unit, having a laugh and a joke – we were just happy-go-lucky lads and we went on the pitch and did the business.' He felt that this probably helped the players cope and you can see his point – certainly that side could never be accused of choking when it most mattered.

Robson's and Bobby Ferguson's organisation of the team was a huge part of this too. Fifteen years later Robson pointed to the fact that they had a 'system to suit every single player in the squad' and that 'everyone knew their job'. This organisation dovetailed with the togetherness of the players – it's doubtful that either would have worked without the other. Robson cited that the squad included 'a lot of individual technique and skill' as well as players who had the 'character and attitude' that was necessary not only to complement those technical abilities but also to cope with the sheer physical demands of such a long season and the extraordinary variances in styles against which they competed.

In addition to the established stars, this team created some new ones.

Alan Brazil was certainly one. Although he had emerged the previous season, his partnership with Mariner and his all round contribution seemed to blossom before our eyes in 1980/81. I have never seen a striker better in a one-on-one situation with a keeper. When Brazil broke past the last defender the net was already practically rippling such was the certainty we felt from the terraces. He was more than predatory – he scored goals from distance as well as from deep in the box but they all had in common that single-mindedness that all the best strikers have when they see a sight of goal.

Eric Gates was another – the little Geordie's slight frame didn't give defenders any advantage whatsoever because his speed and trickery more than made up for it (there must be a stat somewhere of how many penalties we won from lumbering defenders trying to get near him with desperate lunges). Beyond that, he was more creative than he was probably ever given credit for because his contribution to other people's goals was hugely important quite apart from his own impressive tally (fourteen that season). Although Gates had emerged over the previous two seasons, his role (particularly in the European run) was now a firmly established feature of the new shape team centring on the Dutchmen.

Both Gates and Brazil were now internationals – they had well and truly arrived.

Two league defeats (at Leeds and WBA) were not ideal

preparation for the home leg of the UEFA Cup semi-final against Cologne (who included both Tony Woodcock and Pierre Littbarski) but Robson was, as ever, focused and meticulous in his preparation. He later recalled that his approach to Cologne was based on the fact that 'German football is tough – they're difficult to beat and they don't give much away'. He was looking at a likely more cagey affair than the previous round against the flair of the French and he was right, describing the first leg as a 'tough game' with 'not very much in it'. It was however a game we won and in which we kept a clean sheet – Wark the scorer in a 1-0 win.

The games continued to come thick and fast. Just three days later came the FA Cup semi final against Manchester City at Villa Park. The recent introduction of extra-time couldn't have been less welcome for Town and the fact that it was used at the end of ninety goalless minutes on April 11th no doubt contributed to the negative result as Paul Power's quality free kick decided the game.

Part one of the treble was gone – so too was the prospect of Kevin Beattie ever returning as a regular because he broke his arm in the City semi-final and he was never to play again for Town.

For most of us, the pain of defeat was softened by the anticipation of the other two potential prizes and the immediacy of big games pretty much constantly on the horizon. That's not to say that losing a semi-final didn't hurt but we knew that defeat was in no way the end of the season for us.

This optimism could not have been better illustrated by the fact that just three days later we went to Villa Park and took the two points that we thought might end up being the critical difference between Town and Villa as the two clubs looked destined to compete for the title. It was an astounding result under the circumstances and the fact that Brazil and Gates were the scorers once more reminded us that the future still had much potential.

Two defeats (including one at Carrow Road) however immediately followed and once again provided anything but the perfect preparation for the second leg of the Cologne semi final in Europe but no one was brooding too much on the potentially catastrophic impact on our league ambitions because there was work to be done over ninety minutes to make the club's first European final.

Robson's ability to organise and motivate was quite clearly of massive importance in this season more than most. He was forced to change players, formations, tactics and styles for a range of reasons and he needed all of the players to respond. Over the years, compliments about his management style have abounded (Alan Shearer for one considering his man-management skills to be 'second to none' – whether he's dealing with a 16-year-old kid or a superstar he knows how to get the best out of him') but those skills can rarely have been as tested as during those few weeks of this particular season. Terry Butcher said that Robson just 'made you feel a special guy – you feel like you want to go through a brick wall for him' and Paul Gascoigne later recalled from his England days that 'when he talks you listen and you walk away feeling very positive'. Undoubtedly there were techniques behind this but at the heart of it was the man himself.

Preparing his team for the second leg of the UEFA Cup semi-final - with a recent FA Cup exit and a league campaign suffering potentially fatal jitters – needed all his special talents. He was not alone though. Amidst all of the euphoria of the changing rooms after the St Etienne game was the steady and quiet voice of captain Mick Mills saying that 'it's important that we keep our years to the day since the Wembley Cup Final) to see a performance and a 3-0 result that was everything we could have hoped for. Robson was fulsome in his praise for both players and crowd – 'there were two teams in the stadium that night, one on the pitch and one in the stands' - and he felt that 'we had the cushion that we thought would see us safely through'. Despite this feeling, Mick Mills' words of caution on that night in Paris in the quarter final were once again most prophetic – the job was far from done.

Robson though enjoyed the moment and enthused that 'we played magically', producing 'exceptionally good football' at a 'pace that they couldn't master'. There was no doubt about that – the fact the goals came from centre forward (Mariner) and midfield (Thijssen and Wark – inevitably) once again emphasised the all round strength of the side and the fact that all responsibilities were shared. Robson was triumphant – 'I think we murdered them. That's the best of Dutch football and we've blitzed it'. His pleasure was underlined by the fact that this was Town's 65th game of the season.

The press seemed to agree. The Telegraph's Donald Saunders felt that Town could 'look forward with some confidence to their visit to Amsterdam' based on a performance that featured Muhren and Thijssen's ability to outwit their compatriots in midfield and the 'admirable calm' of Steve McCall. Unusually too he pointed out the heavy tactics employed by AZ including tackling that was 'usually heavy, often late and frequently from the back' most often aimed at Mariner and Gates. Saunders' view was that these tactics emphasised AZ's limited ambitions for the first leg – to keep the score down rather than to play. Their game plan was thrown out of the window and necessitated a drastic rethink for the second leg.

Over the previous years, we had learned much about two legged

European ties and had disproved the theory that a significant home advantage was always enough to see you through. No one – fan, player or management – was ready to make that mistake again. Although the manager realistically pointed out that keeping a clean sheet had been 'vital' and his captain admitted that the three goal advantage was more than they'd expected, both knew that the job was not done and Mills emphasised that AZ would be 'better in the second leg'.

How right he was. Robson described AZ's onslaught in the return leg simply as 'a whirlwind'. Playing just two at the back, the Dutch sent everyone forward at pretty much every opportunity. Despite the cushion of an early Thijssen goal to make the aggregate 4-0 at the time (at which point Robson later recalled saying to himself 'I'm going to enjoy this'), this barrage was to take its toll. 'They threw everything at us that any football team could have' Robson later explained – and it worked.

In Robson's words 'they scored and scored and scored; they were unrelenting and we could hardly get the ball'. Robson's admiration for the Dutch League Champions ('they played wonderful attacking football and were a top class team') was significant both because of his later career at PSV and of course the fact that a very important element of his rebuilding at Ipswich had been based around the acquisition of Muhren and Thijssen. This time however he had to play and beat them at their own game.

Once again, the key moment belonged to John Wark who managed to snatch a late header to stem the Dutch flow so that the final 2-4 loss on the night still enabled a 5-4 win on aggregate. This wasn't a night of Town playing flowing exhibition football in Europe (although we had had a few of those in the campaign) – it was a victory for dogged determination. It was, in Robson's words, a 'wonderful end to a pretty marvellous season.' The cup was ours.

In these days of cagey finals which are rarely any sort of spectacle for fear of failure, it is hard to explain the drama of this game even when looking at the scoreline. Over two legs it was real blood and guts. There was simply no time for being circumspect or cautious – it required courage and commitment which were attributes that manager and players at Ipswich Town had in reserve and they needed it because their opponents had them too.

Celebrations back home for the players were delayed slightly when their bags were searched for several hours by Customs officials at Norwich Airport. The suspicion was that this was some Canary mischief; who knows what they expected to find but, had they come across the trophy, they'd certainly have been hard pressed to identify such a thing.

There could be few more significant moments to reflect on the enormity of Robson's achievements than right then. Just three years after lifting the FA Cup he had rebuilt a team and a system and now was holding arguably an even greater piece of silverware.

The 1978 team had been remoulded – the central defensive partnership replaced by one of similar and exceptional resilience, the midfield remodelled away from being driven by traditional English engine room (Talbot and Osborne had departed) towards a more creative and ball playing version via the Dutchmen. Amidst all of these changes he had carefully and skilfully maintained some stability by ensuring that half of the defence remained stable – in the form of Mills and Burley – in front of the ever dependable Cooper in goal and he had ensured that Mariner retained his central importance up front albeit aided and abetted by the new star in Alan Brazil.

A few years earlier it would have been impossible to imagine a Town side without Whymark, Woods, Osborne and Talbot. In

1981 the UEFA Cup Winners wore the Suffolk blue and included none of them. Rebuilding operations don't come much more successful as was evidenced by the wild jubilation that followed. Alan Brazil recalled the open top bus parade by observing that he'd 'never seen so many fans in one place. There were people clamouring up lamp posts and perilously hanging out of their office windows. I felt elated.' He wasn't alone.

If there was one player who epitomised the line between old and new it was John Wark. His quite exceptional talent for arriving in the box at the right time contributed to an absolutely amazing goal haul of fourteen in Europe – a record unlikely to ever be beaten. Across the season though his total was thirty six including a top scoring performance of eighteen in the League.

The fact that Wark had been central to the 1978 team as well as the 1981 team speaks volumes both for his talent and for Robson's appreciation of the importance of blending athleticism and technique because Wark had been as critical a presence alongside Talbot as he was alongside Thijssen.

Wark himself saw 1981 as his best season and certainly it showcased his unique goalscoring abilities better than any other. His manager was fulsome in his praise almost fifteen years later, describing Wark as 'a great box-to-box player' who 'scored goals every season guaranteed' but also 'worked very hard in midfield because he was a defensive midfielder too.'

As supporters, we were to appreciate this even more when Wark returned many years post Robson to take up a key role at the back. Most importantly, the fact that he contributed so many goals was the result of the certainty that the whole team had in his role and ability. In Robson's words 'we knew what we had to do – get the ball into certain situations in wide positions and get crosses for John to come on and make runs in front of Gates and between Mariner and Brazil and score goals'. That's exactly how it worked and if we could see it so too could the opposition – they just couldn't stop it. He was incredible and Robson used this as a key element of his system which was never better exemplified than in 1981.

The pleasure of achievement ran deep for Robson. He knew – as we all did – that the quality of side that he had consistently built deserved more in terms of honours so maybe that night in Amsterdam in May 1981 went some way to redressing the balance. Certainly Robson and the players knew the enormity of the achievement and Robson rightly pointed out that they had had to knock out six teams from six different countries on the way. This mastering of so many different styles, temperaments, climates and rhythms was a real measure of success and provided Robson with, at the time, his 'sweetest moment in club football'.

One of the many plaudits received by the team that season stood out for me – Johnny Rep commented after his St Etienne side had been defeated that 'Ipswich are very clever – they play with their head'. How many times has such a compliment been made about a British side let alone by such an accomplished player? This Ipswich team was though in its manager's image – a man with a vision but also a hunger for learning and competing that was always destined to take him way beyond our shores.

In retrospect, Robson is certain that the 1981 team was the best that he built (international plaudits such as Adidas/France Football magazine's 'European Team of the Year' award tended to back this up). Based on a combination of maturing home grown players (hence the link with 1978), buying well and continuing to develop the Youth scheme, he believed that the side played 'the type of football that hadn't been seen here for many years – not just in Ipswich but in England'. Almost fifteen years later he remained convinced that in 1981 Town were the 'best team in England' playing 'lovely effective football' and getting in 'where it hurt'. He was of course bang on because the success of the side was not solely about the visionary decision to bring in the Dutchmen – it was the blending of the English and European styles that produced flowing and clinical football.

Robson's confidence was shared pretty much universally. Nowhere was this better illustrated than when the winners of two prestigious awards were announced for the 1980/1981 season –

PFA Player of The Year

Winner = Wark

2nd = Thijssen

3rd = Mariner

Football Writers Player of the Year

Winner = Thijssen

2nd = Mills

3rd = Wark

Such a clean sweep for one club never happened before or since.

And we really appreciated it. Robson later acknowledged a 'great love and depth of feeling by the [Ipswich] public for these players – people loved us' and 'we made people sing'. Without the media coverage back then, maybe the rest of the country wasn't quite as aware of an English club achieving so much as they are now but the enormity of the moment certainly reverberated around East Anglia and it is great to know that Robson appreciated that the fans 'understood us'. This, to me, is a telling phrase. Success was hard earned and the reshaping, although relatively fast, wasn't achieved without some poor results and the departure of some popular players but the fans stuck with it and always appreciated their role. Mr Robson and the Cobbolds inspired that.

Once again, Robson's admirers were never far away with offers. It was Sunderland whose chairman allegedly offered to double Robson's considerable salary; the Town Board again said no. Manchester United also made an offer shortly after Town won the cup in Amsterdam and were met with a similar response. This time though with a marked difference. Patrick Cobbold said that the only way that the Board would consider releasing Robson from his contract would be for the England job.

The Telegraph's Bob Oxby, profiling Robson in the programme notes for the F.A. Cup Semi-Final three years earlier, had said – 'In 1962 Alf Ramsey left Ipswich to become the England manager and the signs are that history will repeat itself. When Ron Greenwood finally relinquishes control of the England team, where could the F.A. find a more obvious successor than at Ipswich?' Most of us knew on that night of European glory that that day may be fast approaching.

ON THE MAP

That One Job

As the 1981/82 season dawned players and supporters were focused equally on the glory of achievements last season and the disappointment of what slipped away. We all knew that we should have had a greater trophy haul but took it as a measure of the progress of the club that we could harbour any disappointment in a season that yielded the UEFA Cup.

We knew that on August 29th 1981 the new season would kick off with a home game against Sunderland and less than a month later we would begin the next European adventure in a campaign to retain the UEFA Cup. Exciting times.

Off field commercial activities also started to take the shape that we now know and 'love'. Pioneer became club sponsors in a deal worth £400,000 over three seasons and some of the money was used to fund the building of a new stand that would add almost 5000 seats and would bear the sponsor's name. Shirts too would become portable ad positions for the Hi-Fi giant unless the game was televised in which case the TV companies (commercial as well as BBC) insisted on such blatant commercialism being removed! How quaint this seems in an age when clubs would have every inch of a player's kit sponsored from their studs to their headband if they could.

The league season started positively with a seven game unbeaten run (including a 2-0 win over Liverpool) and plenty of goals especially for Brazil, Wark and Gates. Although a 3-4 defeat at Southampton in early October ended the run, Town still managed seven wins from the next ten to once again be amongst the leading runners by the turn of the year.

The shape of the team was largely familiar. Although some new faces arrived – including David Barnes from Coventry and Tony Kinsella from Tampa Bay via Millwall – they made little impression on the core of the squad. The notable changes were largely the result of injuries. One such was the absence of George Burley – for so long an ever-present – who did not return to the side (having missed probably half of the previous season) until late November. Importantly too, Frans Thijssen suffered a stress fracture to his shin bone that ended his season in February having already missed eight games up to the middle of January. Paul Mariner was also missing from February to April and was largely deputised by Mich D'Avray. Both Mariner and D'Avray had relatively modest returns so it was a good thing that Brazil carried on where he had left of – finishing the season with twenty eight in league and cup (including all five against Southampton in a 5-2 win) followed by the ever prolific Wark with twenty three from midfield - amazing.

Probably the most significant – and certainly the most dramatic – injury was that of Terry Butcher whose season was decimated by a broken nose and severed artery in the bridge of the nose which was so serious that the unstemmable loss of blood at one point seriously threatened his life. The injury happened in an FA Cup tie at Luton on January 23rd and Butcher did not return to the side until the middle of April (Kevin Steggles once again performing an important supporting role in the interim).

Needless to say it would have to be a serious injury to keep the big man out of an Ipswich Town shirt and it certainly was.

Following treatment in Luton after the game, Butcher was transferred to an ENT specialist unit in London where the situation improved very little and constant blood transfusions were needed to replace the ongoing losses. Butcher's weight loss and gaunt appearance must have been alarming for himself and his family especially for a man so physically strong. Eventually an operation put in place pins beneath the cheekbone to tie off the arteries.

Despite a strong league campaign, the potential of a treble like the previous season was never likely to be repeated in 1981/82. Terry Butcher says that 'the problem was that we never truly believed that we were going to win the title as Liverpool surged on.' This is an alarming admission and maybe hints at some waning motivation in the dressing room but the fact remains that Town were still one of a two horse race for the League. Despite ignominious exit from the FA Cup at Shrewsbury in round 5 and the UEFA Cup campaign ending at the first hurdle with a 2-4 aggregate defeat to Alec Ferguson's talented Aberdeen, we were still pushing for the top. A longer run was enjoyed in the League Cup which bought a sniff of Wembley until the prospect was removed by eventual winners Liverpool in a 2-4 defeat over two legs in the semi final (the club's first in this competition).

The League Cup campaign ended in early February following a hard on the heels of a disastrous 0-4 home defeat to the Merseysiders which was hardly the form of championship contenders. The fact was though that between the middle of February and the end of the season Town won fourteen games out of twenty two including three runs of three or more back to back wins. This consistency took the chase pretty much to the wire. In the end though the reds took the trophy by four points but it was notable that the gap between Town in runners up position and Spurs in fourth was twelve points. The season had been dominated by two great sides.

THAT ONE JOB

Whilst the strength of squad was cited for the 'failure' to land more than one trophy in the previous season, it had a far more positive role in maintaining the race for a single competition in 1981/82. The squad was certainly fully employed – only three players (Wark, Muhren, and Mills) managed to complete all 55 league and cup games. As a consequence there were important appearances by Laurie Sivell, Tommy Parkin, Mich D'Avray, Irvin Gernon, Allan Hunter, Kevin Steggles, Robin Turner and even veteran keeper John Jackson, signed at the age of 39 as cover for both Sivell and Cooper who were carrying injuries. With the notable exception of Jackson and Hunter, the others were products of the club's youth policy that continued to garner recognition including being the subject of a film ('Robson's Choice') made by Tyne Tees in a season in which the Youth side made the semi finals of the S. E. Counties League Cup and finished runners up in an international Youth tournament in Italy.

The Youth set up had always been, in Robson's words, 'the lifeblood of the club' (he said in 1979 that his advice to youngsters was 'look, listen and learn – and say thanks.') As the first team took on an ever more distinguished look, this became no less marked. For every Thijssen and Muhren there was a Burley and Brazil – the machine worked on.

Chief Scout Ron Gray said in 1981 that 'Nothing gives me greater pleasure than to see my efforts pay off with a lad going all the way to the top' and he had a few at that stage as names like Burley, Beattie, Mills, Brazil, Gates, Wark and McCall all flew the flag for the Youths at the very top. Gray's pleasure was shared, he said, by 'everybody at the club' getting a 'real thrill out of seeing them make the grade'.

The established nature of the Youth scheme at Portman Road was important because it needed to supply teams and squads to come – it needed to provide continuity whoever was at the helm of the club. Before taking on the role of reserve team coach, Charlie Woods won five trophies in his seven years controlling the Youths and the importance of this was lost on no one. Whether or not we all accepted the likelihood of change being in the air, we certainly accepted the possibility so the importance of the back room structures and teams nurtured by Robson took on a whole new significance.

At the other end of the spectrum, 1981/82 was also significant because of the retirement of Kevin Beattie (technically in fact he did play on but only sporadically and at an increasingly lower level). The broken arm that he had suffered in the FA Cup semi final the previous season had in effect been the last straw and the battering that his body had taken through injury – and treatment using cortisone – had taken its toll. Numerous fan polls over the years have placed The Beat at the top and they speak volumes not only for his exceptional ability but for the affection with which he's held.

It's been said numerous times over the years that Beattie was impassable and that he took no prisoners but this was best (and most appropriately) illustrated by a story told by Michael Caine for whom Beattie doubled in the playing scenes of the film 'Escape To Victory'. The film was made in Hungary and featured locals playing the parts of the Nazi's in the game scenes. They liked to give the Hollywood types a few kicks and Caine was often black and blue when he made way for The Beat to take his place but he was always heartened by Beattie's mantra as he ran on to the pitch – 'Budapest General here they come.'

There can have been fewer more honest and dedicated players. Though he was blessed with natural athleticism, stamina and ability, he developed this alongside a single-mindedness that made him a colossus – simply a player who, at his best, made the team function. Robson never forgot it – he famously responded to Coventry's £450,000 offer for the left-footed Beattie with the answer 'that would buy his right leg'.

In the same season, over 15,000 watched Allan Hunter's testimonial against Celtic – the end of an era with the 'bacon and eggs' partnership moving on (Hunter would join Colchester as Player/Manager where he was reunited with Roger Osborne who'd moved there earlier in the season). Robson described Hunter as 'tall, commanding and with a thou-shalt-not-pass mentality' and this proved apt so many times over the years that some of us feared for how we'd cope without it but, by then, the emergence of Butcher and Osman had removed the concern.

Although Hunter and Beattie had been replaced by Butcher and Osman for some time (with the notable exception of a battling performance at the heart of the defence against Liverpool in the League Cup semi-final that season), the veterans' presence around the club and the enormity of their contribution to the Robson rebuild made their departure very significant. They are forever respected and revered amongst the fans.

On paper 1981/82 may have had the look of an 'after the Lord Mayor's show' season but we fans had been fired up by an exciting League Championship campaign in which – once again – we took our place alongside the best. Robson must have felt further disappointment at missing out on that elusive Championship medal which would have made a fitting triumvirate in his trophy cabinet as recognition for a period of unparalleled achievement. It wasn't to be. On the horizon though we could see more opportunities to take on the best, a new ground taking shape, a strong squad and yet another European campaign on the horizon.

First though was a little matter of the 1982 World Cup Finals in Spain which would feature a number of Town players including Mills, Mariner and Butcher for England; Wark, Burley and Brazil for Scotland. Mariner in particular had a storming World Cup campaign scoring in five consecutive appearances throughout the qualification and final stages. England's performances in Spain were presided over by Manager Ron Greenwood whose selection of so many Town players made him popular with us quite apart from the fact that he was a respected and decent man having built quality sides at West Ham before taking on the England job. When we heard however that he had decided to step down after Spain, the implication was obvious. Many of us held our breath.

****

We had all been thinking about the possibility of Ipswich Town without Bobby Robson. The Board's rebuttal of so many clubs' advances over recent years had suggested that this departure might be for one job and for one job only. Indeed, such was Robson's impact that it had been openly talked about over the last ten years – as early as 1973 J. L. Manning commented in the (London) Evening Standard that Robson 'is a very well tuned-in manager and England will need him one day'. At the time he was just four years into his rebuilding of Ipswich Town and was showing some remarkable progress (including conquering Real Madrid in Europe). They were early days however; by 1982 the prospect was very much more realistic.

Of course we knew by then that his success had been noted all over Europe and that he had so far always resisted the continuous courting by clubs from home and abroad. We also knew that the Board had publicly mentioned the England job and that – passionate patriot that he was – such an offer would be hard for Robson to resist.

THAT ONE JOB

The Cobbolds had long been aware of the fact that their manager was being thought of in national terms – again, in 1973, Chairman John Cobbold stressed that the offer of a ten year contract was sufficient illustration of Robson's importance to the club but that losing him to England would be different' – 'then he is applying his skills to the national effort.' In effect though all of this talk over the years had all been theoretical and would remain so until the job became vacant. Now the possibility was very real. If any job could tempt him away it was that one.

After Ted Croker made the call to Patrick Cobbold the ball was in Robson's court. Cobbold, true to his word, advised Robson of the offer and left him to make up his mind. However, by promising Robson a contract for life and an offer that was considerably better paid than the England job, the wily Cobbold made sure that there was at least a serious option to be considered.

That the England hierarchy were after Robson was an open secret and, long before the offer was officially acknowledged, the rumour mill kicked into action much as it does these days. Robson himself was in Spain watching the World Cup but flew home before the final (well after England's departure) to attend a Board meeting at which many commentators thought he would be resigning. This wasn't quite the case but it seems very likely that he was keeping the Directors up to speed with the ongoing negotiations; quite whether he had 'his people' driving them as would be the case these days is not recorded. In the early part of July 1982 the papers seemed primed to make the announcement and, in the meantime, fed us snippets of what became the increasingly inevitable.

The announcement was finally made on 8th July by F. A. Chairman Bert Millichip who had known Robson personally since Robson's playing days at WBA. In his press announcement, Millichip made clear that this long term knowledge combined with Robson's record at Portman Road made him the natural choice - 'we didn't consider anyone else for the job. We picked our man and we went for him.'

In a move that has uncomfortable parallels with today, Robson's appointment was seen as a turning point not just for the national senior side but also for the wider game from schoolboys through to the Football League. Allen Wade, the then Head of Coaching at the FA was made redundant in a move which was seen as ensuring that the new manager would be able to take the game as a whole by the scruff of its neck. Quite whether any of this was engineered by Robson or was part of the deal that he had been negotiating is unknown but there had been suggestions that Wade's support of Greenwood had been far from wholehearted so it seems likely that there would have been interest in change from a number of quarters.

In any event, Millichip hoped that the new regime would 'introduce greater skills' across the board and Robson too stressed the importance of planning ahead when he said that 'if we want to win the World Cup then we must educate correctly footballers of the highest quality'. The implication of the change of course was that we had not been doing so. The press certainly suggested that the re-organisation was some sort of coup and saw Robson as the only 'victor in any power struggle at Lancaster Gate'. Much of this still sounds very familiar. Whatever structural changes were instigated in Robson's time and since, the continuing under achievement of a national team from the country with the wealthiest league continues to produce calls for fundamental changes at grass root level.

Robson said that leaving Ipswich was a 'terrific wrench' and 'the hardest decision' of his career. His heart, he said 'would always be here'. One of the reasons was that, in his words 'I was loyal to them and they were loyal to me – the sort of relationship that transcended the usual employer-employee set up'. This of course is bang on. In 1973 Robson had said that 'if I'm not still at Ipswich when I'm 50 it won't be because anyone has broken his word. We're not that sort of club' (Robson once described John Cobbold as a man who goes 'around making people happy').

From the beginning, both parties had respected each other and resisted the temptation to change. The time that this afforded was to the benefit of the club and was the basis of much of the subsequent success – at the time of taking on the England job Robson was the longest serving manager in the league. That said, every relationship has its time and Robson acknowledged that he and his family knew very well that he may regret it for the rest of his life if he didn't have a go. He knew that he'd have to trade 'security, contentment, happiness' together with total control of a top club, a supportive Board and the offer of financial security against a very uncertain return from a frequently thankless job.

Robson was looking forward. His five year contract at a salary of £70,000 (which, the press pointed out, was £40,000 more than a Cabinet Minister and £30,000 more than an Admiral – some things don't change), was reward for what he'd done to qualify for the chance but he knew that he would earn it once in the job.

Patrick Cobbold tried to hang on to his manager as an unpaid consultant even going as far as suggesting that Robson would advise the new manager on transfer decisions. The F.A. politely gave this short shrift – they may have accepted that Robson would remain (in Cobbold's words) a 'father figure' at Portman Road but they made clear that he would not be a very active one. It's hard to avoid the suspicion here that the Town board were being somewhat unrealistic but we can put it down to a long term attachment – plus maybe some commercial nous in trying to blag some unpaid advice from the best qualified man to give it. In any event, Cobbold emphasised that Robson would be welcome back at Portman Road at any time and he also didn't miss the opportunity to make a small ticket office plug by pointing out that 'he will have the chance to see as many international players at Ipswich as anywhere else.'

And so it happened. Bobby Robson left. As I recall there was absolutely no supporter backlash (the same could be said of the departures of Terry Butcher and Matt Holland in later years – both absolutely exemplary servants of the club). Everybody understood just what Bobby Robson had done for the club and its achievements under his stewardship. Indeed, we were proud that Ipswich became the only club ever to provide England with two managers –as it turned out, the two most successful. Millichip publicly acknowledged this when he said at the time of the announcement – 'we felt embarrassed talking to Ipswich Chairman Patrick Cobbold taking his club's manager for a second time but he took it in very good spirit.'

Robson had undoubtedly earned the opportunity and few supporters around the country could have been better aware of his qualifications – his tactical knowledge, his motivational strengths (Terry Butcher says that the hairs on the back of his neck still stand up when he thinks about the affect of Robson's personal pep talks on him), his hunger and enthusiasm to take on new challenges (most importantly illustrated by the desire to match foreign systems and players) and his patriotism which was always a driving force. To many, he was the only man for the job (Mr Clough's idiosyncrasies probably doing for his own claims despite his extraordinary talent and track record) and we

THAT ONE JOB

therefore had to accept it regardless of the cost to us. The club that he left was HIS club – its methods, ethos and facilities built up by him but solid and established for others to take on.

The East Anglian Daily Times put it very well when noting the fact that six Town players were in Spain in the England World Cup squad with two more on standby. Alongside the fact that they all played for a side capable of challenging for the League Championship and European honours, this was a measure of how 'what once would have been unbelievable [now] comes to be taken for granted'. Robson ('the best possible choice' for England') and his team had achieved this.

A key member of that team who sat alongside Robson on the touchline throughout many great times was Bobby Ferguson who was immediately announced as the new manager in an understandable effort to foster continuity. His transition from youths to reserves to first team coach was testament to a long tenure alongside Robson and his importance to the club's achievements. Hard and uncompromising as a player (a rugged defender for Newcastle, Derby and Cardiff), Ferguson's success with the reserves had previously earned him the offer of the manager's job at Millwall which he had turned down explaining that he'd 'played' his 'part in creating the [Ipswich] set up' and that he didn't therefore want to 'give it up'. His loyalty was rewarded many times but none more than on that night in Holland in 1981.

Ferguson, an ex-army PT instructor, was a tough disciplinarian whose methods kept the players on their toes – few would speak warmly of him in the same terms as were used for Robson but there was clearly plenty of respect. The issue was whether or not that was enough to fit into the shoes of the departing Robson even though this was Robson's recommendation to Patrick Cobbold.

Some rare signs of acrimony followed Robson's departure – Ferguson claiming greater responsibility for some of Town's successes as well as blaming Robson for some of the subsequent financial problems caused by the building of a new stand. This was a great shame because Ferguson was rightly acknowledged as an important part of the achievements of the period and that ought to have been enough. In 1979 Robson described one of his greatest dislikes as 'people with short memories' so it must have hurt him a little that some of these comments came from someone who might have been accused of having that very problem.

It seems to me that Robson had generally been very conscientious about acknowledging the importance of everyone involved with the club. Ron Gray, Ferguson, Charlie Woods, Cyril Lea, Brian Owen and Tommy Eggleston had all been recognised as important elements of the Robson programme at Ipswich but it would be ridiculous to underestimate the degree to which the rebuilding of the club was driven by one man.

As the dust settled, many of us had cause to look back on just what a man.

Brian Talbot's keyword in describing Robson is 'clever'. He considers that Robson's consistent creation of good teams (at Ipswich and everywhere else) was about 'good judgement.' Part of this was listening to his coaching staff – for example it was they who apparently came up with the tactics in the 78 cup final to stifle service to Brady - and making sure that the back room was a team as well as the players. Bryan Hamilton emphasises the same point, citing Ron Gray as the man who found the young talent and Robson as the one who 'encouraged them and gave them their chance'.

One of the beneficiaries of that support was John Wark who

simply describes Robson as 'the best' and speaks warmly of how Robson 'treated me like a son; I learned a lot as a player and as a person from him'.

George Burley expressed pretty much the same sentiment as he credits Robson with a role much greater than that of manager – arriving in Suffolk at the age of 15, Burley said that 'Bobby Robson bought me up as a person not only a player.'

There could have been few better mentors. It is a measure of Robson's subsequent scale of success that very similar sentiments have been expressed decades later by the likes of Ronaldo, Figo (who said that 'he taught me that life is not just about the good things; sometimes the bad moments you learn from.') and Van Nistelroy (who considered one of Robson's greatest virtues to be that 'he was always there for other people').

Terry Butcher's opinion of the man changed little from the day that he signed his first professional forms in Robson's office at the age of seventeen – he says that 'I thought he was a wonderful guy then and I still do to this day.' The two of them went through a great deal at Portman Road and then with England so this speaks volumes.

Robson never forgot his roots and this level headedness (passed down from his parents) was at the heart of the way in which he treated players. It is telling that Robson once took John and Patrick Cobbold along with other members of the Board to a pit in Derbyshire to show them 'the other side of life'. Similarly, the shock that he suffered on being fired as a young man at Fulham not only offended his sensibilities but remained an example of how not to do things that he kept close to his heart – it was key to his appreciation of the way that he was treated by the Cobbolds and the Ipswich board. The common approach between Robson and the Cobbolds was part of the uniqueness of the era felt by most who experienced it – Paul Mariner recalled that 'from the supporters all the way up to Mr John, the chairman, it was a fantastic period in my life.'

The many warm words from ex players may not suggest that Robson was a disciplinarian. In fact he has always been known as a stickler for smartness and punctuality – probably because both are a sign of respect. His regime was also backed up by men with similar beliefs – Ferguson and Woods for instance – whose methods may have been somewhat more direct.

These techniques generally worked but not in all cases. It came as something of a shock to me to read that Trevor Whymark – a real hero of the Robson years – was not a fan of his manager's motivational tactics employed on some of the youngsters (including Whymark) who he inherited when joining the club. This group was, in Whymark's words, 'taunted' with comments like 'you should be sweeping the streets or cleaning toilets'. Whymark was sure that it was an example of reverse psychology but was equally sure that it would not work in some cases. His respect for Robson's subsequent achievements is crystal clear but it has not changed his views of his early methods. These do not however appear to be widely held concerns since other members of that youth group included Clive Woods, Roger Osborne and Mick Lambert whose recollections of their manager are far more equivocal.

Indeed the general respect and warmth shown by his players is testament to the fact that this discipline was backed up with his legendary man management skills – the sort of closeness that earned respect from players throughout his career. Robson though expected players to behave – to appreciate their position and to earn respect. He treated them hard but respected their response.

In his long career, Robson will have seen many changes but few will have been quite as striking as the shift in power that has enabled players to apparently live by different rules by virtue of their talent and celebrity. This is almost certainly not to his taste but he has said many times that he does not begrudge players their mega salaries these days as long as they perform and meet their responsibilities. In 2008 he compared Britain's sporting heroes, Olympic Gold medallist Rebecca Adlington and World Formula One Champion Lewis Hamilton, to the modern footballer who is 'mollycoddled from such a young age, they seem to lose perspective on life which is why they can appear aloof, badly behaved and spoilt.' In Sir Bobby's view, the comparison wasn't flattering in the eyes of the public. He was of course bang on. Whilst the influence of prima donnas was rarely an issue at Ipswich during his reign, he did have to play Headmaster or Dad in some cases; Butcher, Mariner and Osman apparently being the most frequent recipients of fines for curfew breaking and the like but it never seems to have harmed his relationship with many of the key players of his time. Alan Brazil recalls with some warmth that he was still being admonished for slovenliness by his ex-Manager in 2001 at the age of 42 and having left Ipswich almost 20 years ago. Terry Butcher was always aware that his manager wanted things done 'the right way' and often recalls the slating he took for wearing the 80s fashion statement tee-shirt slogan – 'Fuck Art, Let's Dance.' Such was the mutual respect however that these things were put into context. When it came to playing for the shirt they never forgot their inspiration.

Few people in football know Robson better than Don Howe. Thirty years ago he said that 'it's been a firm friendship since the day we met' and Robson echoes that sentiment to this day. The two had been players together and made the move into management in parallel so their views of footballers from both sides of the fence are to be respected. In Howe's view, the two men shared conscientiousness about training and an interest far beyond playing so their roles in management/coaching were mapped from those early days. Thirty years ago, Howe attributed much of Robson's subsequent success to 'fantastic dedication and enthusiasm for the job' which Howe was certain was unique – 'only he could have done what has happened at Ipswich.' It's unbelievable what he's done not just for the team but for the club and indeed for the town'. Lawrie McMenemy agreed with Howe – in 1979 he cited the club's 'respect throughout European football the achievements of the team and the impossible task of bringing the FA Cup to Suffolk' is down to 'one man'. This book can neatly be summarised as an underlining of this sentiment some 30 years later. In 2008 Don Howe was lending his experience in the background to help Jim Magilton – a choice that can't have been entirely coincidental.

The appreciation of his peers for his achievements at Ipswich was widespread and telling – indeed to this day Robson is one of only three managers to have been made life Vice-Presidents of the League Managers Association.

Even before the great UEFA Cup Win - on the occasion of his 10th anniversary at Ipswich - the club accorded Robson a testimonial match in which, most appropriately, an England X1 (under Ron Greenwood) were the visitors to Portman Road. Managers from across the game queued up to have their say. Terry Neil described Robson as 'a wonderful advert for our game' not only for his successes but for the way that he had achieved them. Jimmy Adamson of Leeds described Robson's achievement at Portman Road as 'one of the most unique in the annals of English football' not just for developing and keeping a team at the top but also for development of the ground and the club overall. Tony Book of Manchester City emphasised that

Robson 'has the respect of every manager in the country and none of us can ever treat his side lightly; he is a man full of ability, honesty and sincerity'. Keith Burkinshaw at Spurs simply felt that Robson 'epitomises all that is good within the game'. Everton's Gordon Lee was very specific about Robson's attributes as a Manager – ' his deep thinking ability as a coach and tactician and his shrewd business sense as an administrator'. Coventry's Gordon Milne also appreciated Robson's achievements at a club of comparable size – 'They [Ipswich] are an example to many clubs of how to be successful on a small budget.'

Success on the field was built on a firm belief in hard work and playing the game the right way. Just four years into the Robson reign, Mick Mills told Steve Curry in the Daily Express that 'there is no doubt that Ipswich's success is the direct result of Bobby's management. He works the players hard but he has an ardent belief in the way the game should be played and he has enough faith in his own ability to make sure his ideas are put into practice.'

Robson himself expanded on his 'hands on' approach when, in the same year, he told J. L. Manning in the (London) Evening Standard – 'we work on skill and technique development – often morning and afternoon. I'm a bit of a nut case on coaching. It's a manager's most rewarding work. I couldn't get my F.A. Coaching certificate fast enough when I was a player' (a fact confirmed by Jimmy Hill and Don Howe who were playing contemporaries of Robson each with a similar hankering for involvement in the game after playing).

Of course physical fitness has to be combined with tactical awareness to have any effect. In this area, Robson was similarly forthright (as Mills suggested) when he said that 'football must be played only in one direction – forward. When you make a square or a back pass that is because you're not good enough to keep going forward. It's the way to lose.' Robson's mastery of tactics – especially in European and international football – was the bedrock of his success throughout his career when he had to take on differing styles, pace, disciplines and climates but he always produced winners with strategic variants on this core belief.

He was too an articulate communicator – Mick Mills recently made the very pertinent point that in the days before easy access to media there was no opportunity to watch DVDs of the opposition – it needed the manager to explain the intelligence gleaned from scouting in such a way that the game plan could be understood by the players based solely on the word of Robson and his coaching staff. These briefings were both one to one (in the dressing room and out of it) and collective – no stone was left unturned and this is reflected in the players' belief that they knew their job and what was expected of them

Robson simply had to convince players (and coaches, directors etc) of the central premise behind his methods and he achieved this by his own forthright and respectful methods. During his career at Portman Road there were almost no detractors (save for a certain Welsh referee) after those early struggles; in fact throughout his entire career it's difficult to find many more.

The club's youth policy was one of the pillars of Robson's success. The fact that only three of the 1978 FA Cup winning side cost a fee is much repeated and is compelling testimony to its success. Robson never denied that the Youth set up predated him (having been established by Jackie Milburn) but, in Robson's view, his regime 'took it into overdrive and really worked hard to make it pay'.

One of the key aspects of this was the breadth of the scouting network which was to unearth gems from Carlisle (Geddis, Turner and Beattie – all freemen of the town since their exploits with Ipswich) and Scotland (Burley, Wark and Brazil). Ten years after taking over, Robson reflected that 'now our youth scheme is the salvation of the club. Transfer fees have gone mad in recent years and if we had not been so strong at youth level we would really have been up against it'. Thirty years on and the importance of a youth scheme in general – and at Ipswich in particular – remains key amidst a transfer system that long ago left behind 'mad'. It is still at the very heart of the club. Jim Magilton neatly summed it up when he said in 2008 that 'from the moment I first walked through the door at this Football club I have been impressed by every aspect of the club's commitment to producing homegrown talent'. This has survived many threats – mostly financial – but remains a key focus to this day and there can be few greater testaments to the work of Robson and his team.

Although not an every day occurrence, Robson would sometimes take in Youth games played on the practice pitch in the morning of home matches and, in the words of Alan Brazil, seeing him on the touch line 'always gave me a little bit extra in the tank'. So many youths wanted to be at Ipswich because of the quality of set up but also the certainty that the Manager would give them a chance if they were good enough.

Parents too were no doubt reassured by the environment to which they were entrusting their kids. Robson's kindly discipline (backed up Charlie Woods' necessarily rather harder version given the nature of young lads) was key as was Robson's personal involvement. This education too went beyond football. Charlie Woods said that the club set great store by character and attitude and that he saw his job as encouraging both. These virtues were exemplified by the man at the top.

John Motson remembered seeing Robson on Ipswich station at some ungodly hour of the morning (at a time when 'anybody with a sense of proportion and well being would still have been in bed') after a huge game the night before. Motson couldn't quite understand why until Robson explained that he was there to see off the parents of a 'promising schoolboy player who might one day be persuaded to sign for Ipswich'. This attention to detail echoes the great Brian Clough's tenacity and dedication to securing talent at its earliest.

Alongside this commitment to youth development was a no-nonsense attitude to buying players. In these days of 'Director of Football' (and other such unfathomable titles) and labyrinthine structures at top clubs, it's good to reflect on Robson's sound approach to business during his Ipswich days. He had two rules – 1) keep news of the deal away from the press until the ink was dry (to avoid disappointment or embarrassment if proposed deals fell though) and 2) make sure that he personally checked out the player ('I wouldn't feel right paying out money for someone I hadn't seen playing'). This latter point, given the extraordinary array of talent that he had in his scouting team, was yet another example of hands on responsibility – spending as though the money were his own. He is reputed to have made a £1.6m profit (remember this is 1969-1982 prices) on transfers during his 13 year reign which is some record when you consider the quality of players coming in. Robson's guiding role in building Ipswich was total - from business to ground development to youth development.

Lastly - and critically - Robson's concern for, and appreciation of, Ipswich fans was deep. In his early days at the club, he's reputed to have regularly met Town supporters outside away grounds and offered them free tickets and he was certainly always appreciative of the vast majority who stuck with him.

He was however – as you'd expect of someone who tells it like it is – unafraid of clashing where he felt it warranted. During the extraordinary 1980/81 season in which Town were chasing domestic and European honours virtually to the last kick, he was frustrated by what he saw as lacklustre home support and accused the crowd of being 'a bunch of zombies' (he later apologised for his choice of words but defended his reasoning) Did this provoke a mass backlash? Hardly. The London Supporters Club magazine proffered more of an explanation than an argument - that teams were so aware of the strength of the Ipswich side that they simply played to avoid defeat which made the 'expected' win that much harder to come by (the curse of the successful).

There's something in this – as there is in Mick Mills' much repeated comment that, at Ipswich, it is often the team that lifts the supporters rather than the other way around. I doubt though that this is vastly different to many clubs or even within particular parts of the ground. When I moved to the North Stand from the Churchman's (as was) in the 80s it was because I was looking for (and found) the noise and singing that was such a key aspect of the game for me regardless of segregation and fences. The match experience was transformed. That didn't mean that there was silence elsewhere or that the passion and commitment of supporters elsewhere in the ground was any less – it was just a different environment. The later replacement of terraces by seats has changed it once again. There are, and always have been, times though when the crescendo of noise has been breathtaking and that is why going to Portman Road remains a thrilling experience for most of us fans.

Robson was just as quick to offer credit to fans too. We all enjoyed the great times collecting silverware and Robson was in awe of moments like the Corn Exchange homecoming after the

FA Cup win when the streets were lined for miles. He knew just what this meant to everyone because it meant the same to him. Paul Mariner saw the passion of the supporters too – 'from the moment I arrived the fever of the supporters' was obvious he said, describing Town fans as 'as passionate as any supporters I've ever played for.' Robson also saw the loyalty of the fans as being a fitting tribute to that of the players – when the club set up a reunion twenty years after the UEFA Cup win he said that he was 'really proud that they've paid such a special tribute to the team'.

He also made friends of supporters well beyond the club. One of these occasions was related in a story by a Leeds fan who had been on a pre-season tour to Holland and was at the PSV v Leeds game but unable to get in. Robson arrived and stopped to sign some autographs. He asked the supporters why they weren't inside and, when told that no tickets were available and that the Leeds team themselves weren't able to help, Robson immediately persuaded PSV to install some fold away chairs in front of the stand and to provide 30 tickets to the fans outside. The Leeds fan concluded – 'a nice gesture from a nice man and one that bought gratitude from the happy Leeds supporters. They went off chanting 'Robson for England'.

Indeed it was Leeds manager Jimmy Adamson in 1979 who expressed an appreciation of Robson's achievements at Ipswich with the words - 'there are few Bobby Robsons in this world of football'. No - there is only one Bobby Robson.

Afterword – In His Shadow

The Robson years fell during my football obsessed childhood and teens so I was privileged to have lived through them in their glory. I was however twenty when Bobby Robson moved on and I have since spent over a quarter of a century watching the club in frequently entirely different circumstances – often in the shadow of the Robson years.

Strangely, the truth is that I have been closer to the club in these times – I have seen more games, been more a part of the club and even introduced a new generation of Fullers to ITFC. As a kid, I had fewer opportunities to follow the great sides of the earlier Robson years and so my knowledge of them was less first hand than later when I have, at various times, had season tickets and racked up many miles (and pounds) in following them.

Maybe this necessary nostalgia colours my view but I genuinely think not. More likely, we just appreciate the highs more once we have experienced the lows; you need a little perspective to measure the one against the other.

Like many of us who grew up with the club, I have come to associate my affiliation as being about the *way* that the club functions as much as its results. Over the years I have often wondered whether my beliefs were formed by the clubs' (under

Robson and the Cobbolds) or were just coincidental. Whatever, the manner in which the club works has always been important to most supporters and many of the best aspects at Ipswich can be traced back to Robson and the Cobbolds despite the many changes since. Robson himself cites John Cobbold's view of 'love the game more than the prize' as being one of the most important lessons that he learned from his time at the club.

We all want to win but not at all costs. Why are Premiership managers these days simply incapable of admitting when a player dives that it's cheating? A wry smile that says 'it would have been OK if he'd got away with it' doesn't say much for their attitude to the game. It's sad that few argue with the mantra that today's game is so money driven that success at all costs is acceptable. I don't believe that Robson or the Cobbolds would ever have accepted this in a million years – in football or in life in general.

When Town beat Morecambe in the FA Cup in 2001, their then President - comedian Jim Bowen – described us as having played with 'dignity'. I know what he meant. The players did not wildly celebrate their ability to beat a team of non leaguers (at the time) because any Premiership players should certainly have done so. This was quite a contrast to Tottenham whose players did cartwheels after a last minute win against Leyton Orient on the same day. Dignity is a much under used word in football but it was great that it was used about our club – Sir Bobby would have approved.

The temptation to cast aside these beliefs – the last vestiges of Corinthian values from the Cobbolds – has however certainly been in evidence post Robson. There have been times when the need to pull out of a rut has been palpably desperate. Watching some pretty dismal sides struggle over the years has been – as with all fans – the price we pay for the glory. Most real

AFTERWARD - IN HIS SHADOW

supporters understand this cycle and the fact that, by and large, it cannot be escaped unless you go for the glory hunter card in which case you can't really be defined as a supporter in the first place.

A key element of this cycle for a club like Ipswich is the transition from underdog to top dog – and back again. The Robson story was all about building up a small town club to stand alongside the giants of the game. We enjoyed the David and Goliath struggle. But then we became the giant and suddenly found ourselves in the opposite corner. Uncomfortable though that may have sometimes been (and Cup defeat at Shrewsbury was one of the more uncomfortable moments), that's what the 11 v 11 nature of the game is all about. And long may it stay that way.

Unfortunately the downward transition started rather too soon after Sir Bobby passed through the exit door at Portman Road.

In the immediate post Robson years we had little to smile about. Bobby Ferguson was appointed in order to deliver continuity and, though he fought bravely against a team that was dismantling around him, the weight of expectations did him no favours. Robson himself may have contributed to these expectations. When he left he said that 'I feel that I leave behind a very fine club and a very good team. At this present time at the club, there is possibly the best playing staff at any time in my reign. I think that the club can stay where it is at the summit of the football world as long as people work hard and make skilful decisions.'

Pretty soon afterwards that ambition seemed fanciful. Much of the dismantling was down to financial pressures and an inevitable sense amongst some players that things would never be the same again. At least part however was of Ferguson's own making – notably the sale of Mick Mills (possibly too much of a trophy Robson connection?) after a record 741 appearances – an absolute legend.

Whatever the reasons, the results didn't come and league positions slumped – worst of all, there was little flair to cheer on the pitch. For supporters who had become accustomed to finishing in the top six as a matter of course, it was a shock to the system to see finishes of ninth, twelfth and seventeenth being rewarded by the Board with a new two year contract for the Manager in 1985. This may have been an echo of a similarly bold gesture of confidence bestowed on Robson in tough times but there seemed far less evidence on which to base it this time around.

As dismal as much of this may sound, there were moments of high drama – I well remember Ian Atkins' late winner against Oxford late in the 1985/86 season that briefly gave us all belief that we could stave off relegation. In many ways Atkins was a neat illustration of the times as he would hardly be mentioned in the same breath as Beattie or Butcher but his heart was big and no supporter ever doubted his commitment. He was a hero for rather leaner times. Such heroism came to nought though because two further defeats left us adrift of Leicester and Oxford themselves and consigned to the (old) second division. In truth, the Robson years looked like decades ago and there was nothing to be gained from nostalgia at that stage.

If we'd hoped that life in the 'lower leagues' would be more comfortable, we were in for a shock. Although a final position of fifth did qualify us for the old style play offs (which include third, fourth and fifth in the second division playing third bottom from the first), the event proved to be a neat summary of how far we had fallen. Watching from the terraces as the team capitulated in a 1-2 second leg defeat at The Valley (following a

0-0 draw at Portman Road) with Charlton was painful – there was a lack of ideas, cohesion and, worst of all, what looked like a stand up fight between defenders unable to galvanise themselves to grab this opportunity. It was sad and, in some ways, pitiful to watch. It also cost Ferguson his job although technically his contract was not renewed rather than being terminated.

I remember being excited by John Duncan's appointment as successor largely because of his exciting style as a player and the fact that he was making a name for himself in his early managerial career at Chesterfield. Here, we hoped, was a man hungry for success and for whom joining Ipswich was a step up. A skilful player used to flair, he must also have much in common with the way that we liked to see the game played.

How wrong could I have been? It's hard to remember too much to recommend Duncan's stint at the helm – apart maybe from his drafting in of David Lowe and the emergence of Simon Milton whose performances and contributions were rare glimmers of class. Maybe Duncan simply felt that the playing staff were capable only of a fairly long ball game or maybe he wanted to carry on what had worked for him at Chesterfield at a lower level. Either way it was clear that, not only did it not work in the second division (as was), but that the faithful didn't want to watch it. His three seasons at Portman Road delivered three mediocre finishes (eighth, eighth and ninth) and little to shout about. That's a frighteningly easy sentence to write but watching Town over those three seasons was often a much longer sentence.

When John Lyall (assisted by Mick McGiven) took the helm for 1990/91, I was probably one of many who thought that we had struck lucky. A man of great experience (in direct contrast to Duncan), knowledge and obvious decency had come to take over and we believed that he had done so because he genuinely felt that (like 'his' West Ham from which he was cast aside after almost 35 years on the back of relegation in 1989) ours was a club that did things the right way and would give him the time and respect due to sort things out.

Success was not immediate (finishing fourteenth was hardly inspirational and must have been seen as such by one J. Duncan) and the appearance of a slew of ex-Hammers including Steve Whitton, Paul Goddard and even Phil Parkes did little to convince us of a brave new world. Lyall too seemed a little distant from the media and the importance of this relationship was probably stressed by the fact that the same could be said of his two predecessors – but not of Robson. The press had never had a perfect relationship with Sir Bobby but he had always been open and honest; it is likely that Robson simply understood the importance of communication with supporters rather better than most and he has to this day retained a respectful dialogue even after his disgraceful treatment by the very worst tabloid scum during his England tenure.

Lyall's first season turned out to be purely preparatory because his second delivered a championship and return to the big time. Indeed, this was a very different top table that we joined – the newly formed Premier League. At the time few of us could have foreseen the degree to which it would change the whole complexion of the game from grass roots to internationals – we just wanted to be back at the top. Our journey there was a text book case of combining brilliant days with results ground out through sheer persistence. In 1991/92 we proved the maxim that successful sides wins even on days when they plays badly – the team just seemed to have an inexorable momentum in the end.

If we were looking for a sign from the kick off it wasn't obvious.

AFTERWARD - IN HIS SHADOW

The very first fixture of the season at Twerton Park, Bath - temporary home of Bristol Rovers – was a bizarre see-saw of a game that ended 3-3 after Ipswich had been well on top before being pegged back by late goals (one from a certain Marcus Stewart). As the season progressed though it became clear that Lyall had formulated a plan based on some key relationships – Goddard and Chris Kiwomya up front (20 goals between them), Whitton and Dozzell in midfield (another example of experience and youth combining), skipper Linighan and Neil Thompson at the back.

The constant throughout being the one and only Mick Stockwell who (alongside keeper Craig Forrest) had a 100% appearance record in the league campaign that ended with promotion at Oxford United on April 25th 1991. What a day that was. Car journeys to and from the ground were snail's pace as roads were clogged with flags waving and blue and white scarves hanging from vehicles of every description as we edged our way slowly towards what felt like the inevitable. There had been earlier key points too – I remember a last minute winner from Neil Thompson (of all people) hammering a beauty at Southend greeted with mayhem by all of us in the tiny Roots Hall ground.

Not that we were always so confident – being an Ipswich supporter doesn't prepare you for that emotion. As we approached the winning post there were plenty of times when we almost stumbled – a defeat at Bristol City meant a long way home followed by a nerve wrangling scoreless draw with Grimsby in a night match. Both could both have been enough to finish the season but instead it meant waiting till Oxford and of course, as it turned out, no one had any problem with that.

Did any of us believe that we could recreate the consistency of the Robson years? I doubt that we really understood the chasm that was being created between the Premier League and the rest so maybe we did dare to believe that we were back to stay. Naïve? Maybe but early signs were good (we didn't lose a Premier League game until mid September) and the ground shook to the rafters as we beat reigning champions Leeds 4-2 at Portman Road with a stirring display of passion and goals from the new guard – Kiwomya and Dozzell - and two from the great link to the past – John Wark. That day still resonates as almost fairytale stuff and it exemplified the hope of 1992. It was 1993 that delivered the wake up call as we won just four games before the season ended with a sixteenth finish. Our naiveté was the main victim – it became very clear that this was going to be tough and that our ambitions were inevitably going to be far more modest than those of the Robson years.

Lyall's decision to take a step back (or should we say 'up' in terms of his new Directorial – and baffling – job title) meant that McGiven took over coaching duties in 1993/94 and the consequence would be dire. The relative success of the previous year had been based on avoiding defeat – Ipswich had drawn no less than sixteen of their games – and McGiven seemed to take this on as a policy for 1993/94 believing that, with the limited playing staff available, our best hope was to avoid defeat which meant packing the defence and not worrying too much about attacking. The result as a spectacle was obvious.

One writer commented that, if Ipswich were playing in his back garden, he'd pull the curtains. Another reporter accused Blackburn of a crime against football by failing to beat Ipswich in the last game of the season that would have meant our relegation (we survived by a single point.) Frankly, these words hurt and many of us wondered how on earth we could have fallen so far as to be subjected to such – totally legitimate – ridicule.

AFTERWARD - IN HIS SHADOW

In pre-internet days, I can only wonder just how we supporters would have responded to a poll asking us whether we'd rather survive like this or fail by attempting to play. I think that I know. Corinthian it may be (and possibly naïve too) but achieving top status by these methods rankled – there was no pride to be gained.

If any of us attributed the grim days of the previous season to managerial musical chairs we were not to be reassured by the events at the beginning of 1994/95 when Lyall made Goddard and John Wark responsible for coaching whilst McGiven became Football Development Officer. Quite what all of this meant was a mystery to most but what was very clear was that it didn't work and a season that delivered just seven wins in forty two including a 0-9 mauling at Old Trafford was testament to the fact. By then, Lyall and McGiven had departed to be replaced by George Burley. This time the Manager had a job title and task that was very clear – the season was written off and he, like the rest of us, was focused on rebuilding long before relegation was formally decided.

Burley was one of us – as was his Assistant Dale Roberts. In his own words, Burley had 'grown up' at Ipswich and considered Ipswich to be his club – 'I don't care where they are, I want them to do well. I was bought up as a player here. It's my job to try and get them back to where they were in the past.' Echoes of Robson already.

Burley's early managerial career too was beginning to suggest that he might be as formidable a manager as he was a player. He had to withstand some early nonsense between Ipswich and his former club, Colchester (when the latter made an accusation of improper behaviour despite the fact that they had apparently granted Burley permission to speak to Ipswich) but he rode this out as did we supporters although it still seems to be a source of irritation to supporters of the U's to this day. With new Chairman David Sheepshanks at his side, Burley set about ringing the changes in order to wash away all memories of the previous debacle of a season. This involved bringing in some new faces – the most significant of which was Tony Mowbray from Celtic – and promoting some promising youngsters such as James Scowcroft and Richard Wright to the first team. Ipswich has always been a club that believes 'if you're good enough you're old enough' and Burley wasn't about to change anything – Mick Mills recalls that Burley was one of a few exceptional players who almost bypassed the reserves and started to train with the first team when they were just teenagers so he knew the value. This approach largely worked – although seventh place was one off the play offs the season signalled that the massive rebuilding job was underway.

Over the next four seasons, the play offs would be a regular event for us but we learned the heartbreak of failure until we were rather too well acquainted with the skills of dealing with it. Inevitably, these games are amongst the most vivid memories because, at that stage, you feel close enough to smell it but hopes can be wrecked by the slimmest of margins. In 96/97 the away goals rule did for us against Sheffield United. The following year we were strictly second best to Charlton in both legs of the semi (despite having enjoyed a storming run to the play offs partly attributable to Bryan Hamilton's short uncontracted reign alongside Burley) and in 98/99 it was again to be away goals after extra-time to Bolton.

In many ways these were key seasons. Patience was necessary and, though it would be a lie to say that there weren't voices of protest who felt that Burley wasn't making the necessary progress, the vast majority of supporters could see development all over the pitch and right across the club. We knew that we were heading in the right direction and the arrival of Jim Magilton and David Johnson (mark two) combined with the emergence of Kieron Dyer were all major plus points as we pondered falling just short.

1999/2000 changed everything. The team finishing third is always seen as going into the play offs reluctant to be there against opponents who are on a high and raring to go. Maybe though we were fired by a feeling that we should have been first or second (those positions going to Charlton and Manchester City.) Certainly we had nothing to fear based on the fact that we had beaten most of the play off participants (and indeed lost only one in four to the two promoted teams) sometimes by some margin including a 6-1 mauling of Barnsley and a 3-1 away win at Charlton.

Being drawn against Bolton in the semi's also gave us something extra after losing to them at the same stage in the previous season – just part of the recent experience that no other team could match.

In the event the three play off games were amongst the best that I have ever seen. Coming back to draw 2-2 away at Bolton was an effort of sheer steel – we were down and out at 0-2 until Marcus Stewart took the game by the throat with 2 amazing goals that seemed to unleash (or maybe underline) the collective determination to make this the year. At Portman Road in the return, nobody could have predicted what was going to happen- even minute to minute. It was simply a staggering roller coaster of a ride in which we came through 5-3 in a game of hot tempers, sendings off and penalties aplenty. To this day it seems that many Bolton supporters blame referee Barry Knight for their defeat but my view remains the same – the real culprit was Sam Allardyce whose petulant antics spurred on his players to ever greater indiscipline from which we clearly benefited.

Amongst the spats and tantrums, Jim Magilton took the game by the scruff of the neck with a legendary hatrick that took us through on a night when the nerves were shredded by full-time and did not recover for at least 24 hours.

Returning to the old Wembley for the final against Barnsley – the last ever domestic game - and being led by one of the stars of 78/81 inevitably reminded those of us who'd been there of the Robson years. By that stage we all knew that the Premiership had changed football forever and that being outside of it would be subject to the law of diminishing returns. We were all hungry for a return.

Having not been at Wembley in 78, it was for me a memorable day from the time I awoke to the journey home and the congratulatory texts from friends well in to the night. In between was as dramatic a final as there has ever been in what is now widely considered to be the biggest single match in domestic football with a prize much greater than any other. Living through it was tough but, in retrospect, I can now ponder on the amazing parallels with the great cup semi-final of 78 against WBA.

Although we fell behind to a bizarre goal, we then found ourselves two goals ahead and seemed to be on our way when the opposition got back into the game with a penalty conceded by a normally 100% cool and reliable centre half (Mowbray rather than Hunter this time) and there set in a sense of collective fear. Not only that but, had it not been for an absolutely miraculous save by Richard Wright, we would have found ourselves pegged back to level terms. However, when Martin Reuser made it number four we all knew. Amongst the many wonderfully vivid memories of that day (including the sea of blue and white going up Wembley Way and the moment when Tony Mowbray's header hit the net to bring us back into the game) was one that balanced things. Seeing a father with two sobbing young lads, one held by each hand, dressed in red and white reminded me of how we'd suffered crushing disappointment and that inevitably we would do again. Offering a consoling word (a genuine one too – Barnsley had been tremendous that day) wasn't going to make any difference to them at that moment but I hoped that they'd have their day. This was ours.

History will recall that 2000/2001 saw Town back in the big time. A top 5 finish in the Premiership meant qualification for Europe. A team with no big names shocked the glitterati and made friends all over the place. Achieved under the tutelage of one of Robson's boys, the parallels could not be ignored.

The key was togetherness and team spirit that enabled players to play above themselves. Indeed, several of the First Division promotion winners who looked most likely to struggle at the top did quite the opposite and their success was all the more admired.

At the heart of it all was the exceptional Matt Holland – almost a latter-day Mick Mills who was captain material form the day he arrived at the club and whose performances were exemplary in every way both on the field and off of it. His 100% appearance record that season was just ahead of Marcus Stewart, Jermaine Wright and Richard Wright all of whom made justified names for themselves.

How sad then that within a year it would all fall apart – a few injudicious big name (and similarly salaried) signings upsetting the delicate balance of the side and leading to relegation and the removal of George Burley. Whilst few of us felt that our arrival back at the top was a permanent one, we could not see it being so fleeting. We retained great affection for Burley too; whatever went wrong that season nowhere near obliterated his achievement in getting us back to the top and doing it the Ipswich way. The fact that less patience was shown after things started to unravel is probably the best example of changing times and the devastating financial implications of relinquishing Premiership status

The arrival of Joe Royle to follow Burley was not universally popular and this may be one of the reasons that his performance at the club has been – in my opinion - so harshly judged. Relegation allied to the collapse of the ITV Digital deal (which would have generated significant funds) and disappearing 'parachute payments' created a disastrous financial situation and to administration.

Royle was forced to sell every decent player that the club either developed or discovered (including Darren Ambrose and Ian Westlake). Despite this, he made the play off semi's in two of his first three seasons at the club (only missing out by a single place in his first year) which was more than credible. The strain of constantly rebuilding took its toll in his fourth season when a fifteenth finish was the club's worst for forty years. Royle and Chairman David Sheepshanks met in private and agreed to call it a day – to their great credit neither man has ever spoken about what was said behind closed doors which I think is a sign of their dignity to be admired. Indeed, Jim Magilton considers Royle to have been the best manager that he played under as well as being a 'decent bloke' – exactly the impression that I had of him. Few fans seemed to agree; he was often berated for a 'long ball' game that I personally rarely saw at Portman Road. I saw a man trying very hard against the odds.

Royle's appointment had been high profile – an experienced big name manager to take over from the relatively inexperienced Burley. Royle's successor went to the other extreme. Jim

AFTERWARD - IN HIS SHADOW

Magilton had barely walked out of the door as a player at Ipswich before he was invited back in as Manager. There was much speculation at the time as to who would be the new man – the usual suspects being named – but when the rumour started to circulate that the Board were considering Magilton few cannot have been surprised. In his favour was an exemplary record as a player at Portman Road and beyond. Indeed, the greatest compliment that I can pay Magilton the player is that he filled the gap left by Matt Holland. He had gravitas and commanded respect not just for the way that he played but his enthusiasm and energy; players would listen.

He was also very respectful of the club and seemed genuinely honoured to have played for it. It is all the more sad then that his tenure ended amidst disappointment at very modest achievements; his rebuilding was boosted by far greater funds than any of his predecessors and yet consistency of results failed to materialise. Indeed, when his contract was terminated in April 2009, the league table showed won, lost and drawn columns as almost identical – a succinct recipe for mid table. This doesn't alter the fact that he is a passionate club man and that he went about his task with single minded determination and a constant eye on the history and pride of this 'great football club' (a phrase that he regularly used.)

The investment by Marcus Evans – including the appointment of ex British Olympic Association Chief Exec Simon Clegg just one day before the Magilton sacking - has changed people's expectations and had made Magilton's job very different to that of Royle. Although Magilton expressed the same focus on youth, discipline, training and commitment as had been the mantra since Sir Bobby's days, the fact was that a number of (sometimes very ordinary) 'big name' players came through the door rather than youngsters coming through the ranks. This was presumably designed to reap more instant rewards ('you win nothing with kids....') but it was an expensive policy that demanded quick returns. An inevitable sign of the times. Magilton's reign was a good example of football 2009 and it's a tough place. Whatever the ending, all Town fans recognise the importance of Magilton's ten year relationship with the club and a mutual respect will continue.

The arrival of Roy Keane as Magilton's successor was most certainly significant. A big name and a fiery personality with a playing track record at the very top, he is not however an obvious Ipswich character. His arrival at the behest of the club's owner undoubtedly signals a new era.

Should the new man have been looking for some advice or orientation for his role he might have turned to one man.

Sir Bobby wrote just days after the appointment that the new manager needed to take a hands-on approach to finding players ('look at that player carefully over a period of time, research their background, ask your friends in the game and then make your move'). This approach served Sir Bobby well at Portman Road and well beyond.

Another key point was Sir Bobby's acknowledgement that managers no longer have complete control of a club in the way that he did at Portman Road and that Keane's previous manager Brian Clough did at Forest. This means that the manager has to find a way of effectively integrating with the much larger and more fragmented business structure of a modern club. Again, Sir Bobby will have seen this from both sides – from Ipswich to Barcelona - and so few could have had a better informed view.

Sir Bobby – like all Town fans – wished the new man luck. Keane saw his new employer as a' proper football club' and he's right. Sir Bobby echoed the point when saying that that Keane has in his hands 'one of the loveliest clubs in the country' and that if things go well 'Ipswich may be as good to him as it was to me'. Now that is a thought.

****

Hanging on to the past is no good. It was a shock to me that some players in the 90's were apparently determined to resist the move to bring back an ex Robson era player as manager because they were tired of being reminded of the club's illustrious past and felt that the pressure was not only unnecessary but unhelpful. They no doubt argued that the game has changed – of course it has – and might have pointed out that just watching film of those 70s and 80s sides shows this not least because of the sheer pace of the game.

This argument only makes sense in the context of players being temporarily attached to the club – for supporters it's for life. This is why, in my opinion, none of us should ever have any objection to being reminded of the club's past. Indeed, when doing a tour of the ground, it struck me that the walls were adorned with pictures of this and not just from the Robson era but of course from Ramsay's and, much more recently, Burley's. This is all to be celebrated.

And Sir Bobby has always been central. He's remained one of us wherever he's been in the world. When in 2003 Ipswich staged a testimonial for Dale Roberts who tragically died of cancer at the age of 47, there could only be one team to play - Newcastle United managed by Sir Bobby and including Town Youth Academy graduates in the shape of Ambrose, Bramble and Dyer. Roberts had been a youth at Portman Road in Robson's reign – indeed he'd been a member of the F.A Youth Cup winning sides of 1973 and 1975 – and was at the club for six years under Robson. A fellow Geordie, Roberts returned alongside Burley and played a critical part in promotion back to the Premiership and Europe. It was an emotional night made more so by the presence once again at Portman Road of a truly great man.

I didn't write this book to be nostalgic. Like all fans, I spend much time looking forward as the club rebuilds and hopefully heads back to the peak. The context of this though cannot help but be informed by a glorious past. Some fans – often wearing yellow – may criticise us for living in the past but what a past it was. What is far more important for me is the effect of the images, statues, films and history books. All should acknowledge the glory of the Robson years as an INSPIRATION. It's as important going forward for our club as it is looking back. That's quite a legacy.

Robson's Players

During Sir Bobby Robson's thirteen and half years at Portman Road, seventy players appeared in his first team. Below are their record of full appearances under Sir Bobby and in the next column is their full appearances for the club overall

Player	Full Appearances under Sir Bobby Robson	Total Appearances for Ipswich Town
Mick Mills	665	737
George Burley	376	500
Paul Cooper	355	575
Allan Hunter	354	354
Trevor Whymark	321	322
Kevin Beattie	296	296
John Wark	294	670
Colin Viljoen	287	367
Clive Woods	278	278
Paul Mariner	269	339
Russell Osman	258	382
Brian Talbot	227	227
Eric Gates	222	339
Mick Lambert	219	219

Player	Full Appearances under Sir Bobby Robson	Total Appearances for Ipswich Town
Arnold Muhren	214	214
Peter Morris	213	249
David Best	193	199
Bryan Hamilton	186	186
David Johnson	174	174
Terry Butcher	173	350
Colin Harper	161	171
Alan Brazil	160	195
Laurie Sivell	158	175
Frans Thijssen	134	167
Roger Osborne	127	127
Derek Jefferson	115	172
Steve McCall	104	321
Ian Collard	98	98
Jimmy Roberston	98	98
Billy Baxter	89	459
Mick Hill	74	74
Frank Clarke	71	71
Les Tibbot	70	70
Charlie Woods	70	70
Geoff Hammond	64	64
Tommy Carroll	59	124
Mick McNeill	52	168
John Peddelty	50	50
Rod Belfitt	46	46
John Miller	43	43
Bobby Bell	36	37

Player	Full Appearances under Sir Bobby Robson	Total Appearances for Ipswich Town
John O'Rourke	32	72
David Geddis	30	30
Kevin Steggles	30	60
Ron Wigg	27	39
Frank Brogan	26	220
Robin Turner	26	29
Kevin O'Callaghan	24	87
Dale Roberts	22	22
Keith Bertschin	20	20
Pat Sharkey	18	18
Mich D'Avray	16	201
Tommy Parkin	13	61
Danny Hegan	12	230
Terry Austin	11	11
Chris Barnard	8	20
Billy Houghton	8	117
Bobby Hunt	6	18
Ray Crawford	5	354
Glen Keeley	5	5
Irvin Gernon	4	87
Terry Shanahan	3	3
Steve Stacey	2	3
Bruce Twalmley	2	2
Alec Bugg	1	4
John Jackson	1	1
Paul Overton	1	1
John Stirk	1	8

ON THE MAP
Sources & Bibliography

Books & Publications
- 'Bobby Robson – An Englishman Abroad' by Bobby Robson with Bob Harris (Pan Books, 1999)
- 'Farewell But Not Goodbye – My Autobiography' by Bobby Robson with Paul Hayward (Hodder & Stoughton, 2005)
- 'Living The Game – Sir Bobby Robson' by Bob Harris (Weidenfield & Nicholson/Orion, c 2005)
- 'The Essential History of Ipswich Town' by Mel Henderson and Paul Voller (Headline, 2001)
- 'The Men Who Made The Town' by John Eastwood and Tony Moyse (Almeida, 1986)
- 'Ipswich Town – Champions of England 1961-62' by Rob Hadgraft (Desert Island, 2002)
- 'Curse of The Jungle Boy' by Ray Crawford with Michael Wood (PB Publishing, 2007)
- 'The Greatest Footballer England Never Had – The Kevin Beattie Story' by Rob Finch (Cult Figure Publishing, 2007)
- 'There's an Awful Lot Of Bubbly In Brazil' by Alan Brazil with Mike Parry (Highdown, 2006)
- 'Butcher – My Autobiography' by Terry Butcher with Bo b Harris (Highdown, 2005)
- 'Match of My Life – Ipswich Town' edited by Mel Henderson (Know The Score Books, 2008)
- 'Ipswich Town – The 1978 F.A. Cup Story' by Mel Henderson (Breedon Books, 2008)
- Ipswich Town Annual 1977 – complied and edited by Mel Henderson (Circle Publications, 1977)
- 'The Who's Who of Ipswich Town' by Dean Hayes (Breedon Books, 2006)
- Ipswich Town Annual 1979 (Circle Publications, 1979)
- 'By The Book' by Clive Thomas (Collins Willow, 1984)

SOURCES & BIBLIOGRAPHY

- Mick Mills Testimonial Programme 1976
- Laurie Sivell Testimonial Programme
- Paul Cooper Testimonial Programme 1986
- Bobby Robson Testimonial Programme, 1979
- Wembley 78 FA Cup Final Brochure (ITFC)
- One Day In May – 1978 FA Cup Reunion Magazine (Evening Star, 1998)
- Wembley Showdown – Arsenal v Ipswich Souvenir Special (Football Magazine, 1978)
- 'Gunners for Glory' (London Evening News, April 25 1978)
- 'Bobby's Bionic Battlers' (Daily Express Cup Final Pullout, May 6th 1978)
- 'Wembley's Master Gunners' (London Evening Standard, May 1978)
- 1978 FA Cup Final programme
- Various other match programmes

Articles
- 'The Real Bobby Robson' by Steve Curry (Daily Express, 1978)
- 'The Cobbold Dynasty' by Ian Hunnybell (Talk Of The Town magazine, ITFC, 2007)
- 'Do You Remember?' (ITFC Match day programme v Reading, September 2008)
- Sir Bobby Robson On Football column (Mail On Sunday, December 2008 and April 2009)
- Various East Anglian Daily Times and Evening Star clippings from July 1982

Audio Visual
- 'Right Hammerings' (Visionsport International, 1997)
- 'Just Call Me Bobby' – Sir Bobby Robson's Life In Football (BBC Worldwide, 2003)
- 'Boys of 81' (Visionsport International)

- 'Ipswich Town – The Golden Goals Collection' (Watershed {Pictures, 1994)
- 'Match of The Day – Ipswich Town' (BBC Enterprises 1993)
- 'The Official History Of Ipswich Town' (Visionsport International, 2006)
- Radio Orwell Cup Final Celebrations (6 May 1978)

Sites
- www.prideofanglia.com
- www.nufc.com/html/robsonfact.html
- www.cards.littleoak.caom/au

NOTES

Printed in the United Kingdom by
Lightning Source UK Ltd., Milton Keynes
142324UK00001B/33/P